WINERY DOGS
OF NAPA VALLEY

Photography by **Andrea Jacoby & Heather Zundel**

Text by **Elaine Riordan**

Published by Winery Dogs Publishing
Hardcover, Third Edition
First printing June 2008

ISBN: 0-9773041-3-4

Address correspondence or orders to:
Winery Dogs Publishing
sales@winerydogs.com

Individual books may be purchased at:
www.winerydogs.com

Photography by Andrea Jacoby and Heather Zundel
with contributing photography by Jaime Fritsch and Luz Ovalle
See page 232 for photography credits.

Photos © 2005, 2006, 2008 Winery Dogs Publishing
Foreword by Andrea Jacoby
Text by Elaine Riordan

Design by Createffects Inc.
(404) 921-3338

Printed in Korea by Asianprinting.com

Dogs remind us of what we value most: the joy of unguarded affection and the peace of quiet companionship. We dedicate this book to our dogs, past and present, who have given us so much happiness—Mac, Wesley, Mulligan, McGee, Katrina, Jock, Gidget, Ambro, Corky, Casey, Josie, and Pops.

Chu Chu
Darioush

Winery Dogs of Napa Valley

TABLE of CONTENTS

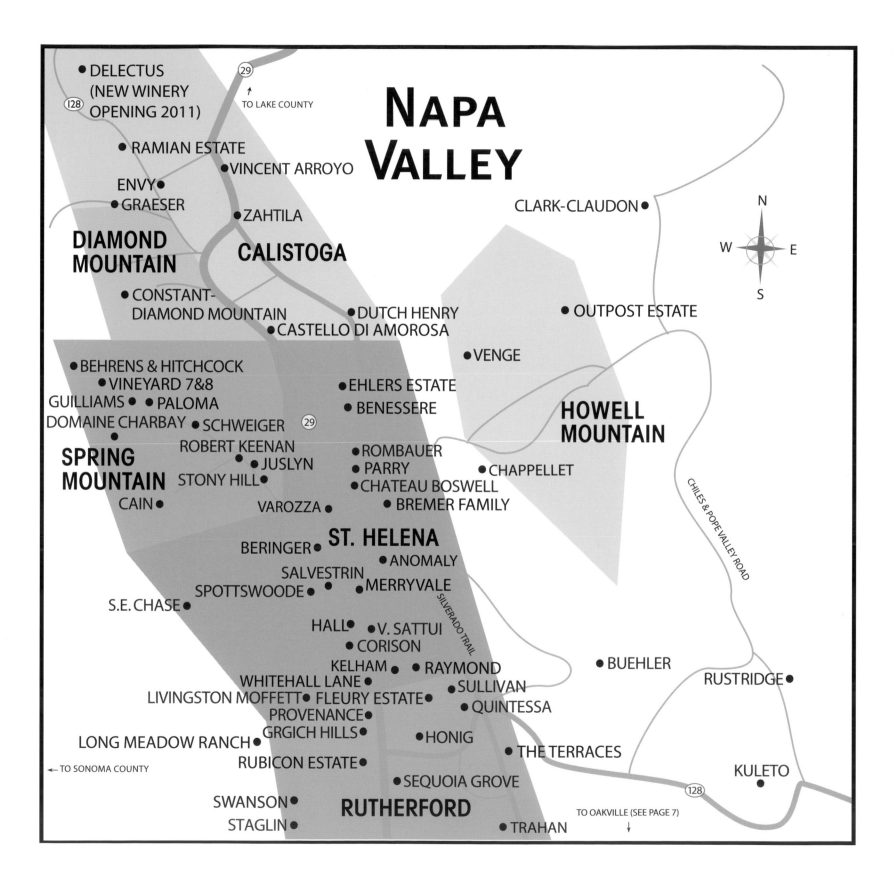

NAPA VALLEY

• DELECTUS
(NEW WINERY
OPENING 2011)

• RAMIAN ESTATE

• VINCENT ARROYO

ENVY •
• GRAESER

• ZAHTILA

**DIAMOND
MOUNTAIN**

CALISTOGA

↑ TO LAKE COUNTY

• CLARK-CLAUDON

• CONSTANT-
DIAMOND MOUNTAIN

• DUTCH HENRY

• CASTELLO DI AMOROSA

• OUTPOST ESTATE

• VENGE

• BEHRENS & HITCHCOCK

• VINEYARD 7&8

GUILLIAMS • • PALOMA

DOMAINE CHARBAY • SCHWEIGER

• EHLERS ESTATE

• BENESSERE

**HOWELL
MOUNTAIN**

ROBERT KEENAN
• • JUSLYN

**SPRING
MOUNTAIN**

STONY HILL •

CAIN •

VAROZZA •

• ROMBAUER

• PARRY

• CHATEAU BOSWELL

• BREMER FAMILY

• CHAPPELLET

BERINGER •

ST. HELENA

• ANOMALY

SALVESTRIN

SPOTTSWOODE • • MERRYVALE

S.E. CHASE •

HALL • • V. SATTUI

• CORISON

KELHAM • • RAYMOND

WHITEHALL LANE •

LIVINGSTON MOFFETT • FLEURY ESTATE •

PROVENANCE •

GRGICH HILLS •

LONG MEADOW RANCH •

RUBICON ESTATE •

SWANSON •

STAGLIN •

RUTHERFORD

• SULLIVAN

• QUINTESSA

• HONIG

• THE TERRACES

• SEQUOIA GROVE

• TRAHAN

• BUEHLER

RUSTRIDGE •

KULETO •

← TO SONOMA COUNTY

TO OAKVILLE (SEE PAGE 7)
↓

SILVERADO TRAIL

CHILES & POPE VALLEY ROAD

N
W + E
S

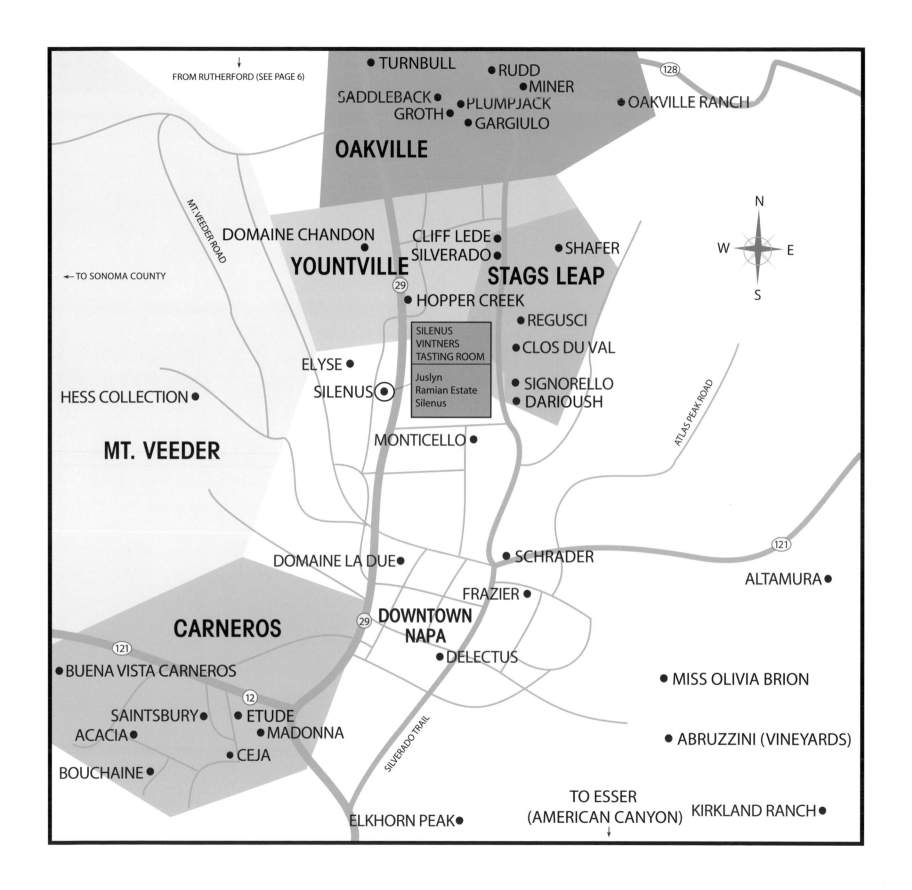

FROM RUTHERFORD (SEE PAGE 6)

• TURNBULL
• RUDD
• MINER
SADDLEBACK •
• PLUMPJACK
• OAKVILLE RANCH
GROTH •
• GARGIULO

OAKVILLE

DOMAINE CHANDON •
CLIFF LEDE •
• SHAFER

YOUNTVILLE
SILVERADO •

← TO SONOMA COUNTY
STAGS LEAP

29
• HOPPER CREEK

• REGUSCI

SILENUS
VINTNERS
TASTING ROOM
• CLOS DU VAL

ELYSE •

Juslyn
Ramian Estate
Silenus
• SIGNORELLO
SILENUS ◎
• DARIOUSH

HESS COLLECTION •

MONTICELLO •

MT. VEEDER

DOMAINE LA DUE •
• SCHRADER
ALTAMURA •

FRAZIER •

CARNEROS
DOWNTOWN NAPA
29

• DELECTUS
121

• BUENA VISTA CARNEROS
• MISS OLIVIA BRION

12
SAINTSBURY •
• ETUDE
ACACIA •
• MADONNA
• ABRUZZINI (VINEYARDS)
• CEJA

BOUCHAINE •

ELKHORN PEAK •
TO ESSER
(AMERICAN CANYON)
KIRKLAND RANCH •

128

121

MT. VEEDER ROAD

ATLAS PEAK ROAD

SILVERADO TRAIL

N
W — E
S

Bodie
Rubicon Estate

Winery Dogs of Napa Valley

FOREWORD

People always say, "Do what you love to do." So my husband, Allen, and I merged two of our passions—wine and dogs—and set out to publish a book about the two. It was also a perfect way for me to indulge a third passion of mine, photography, and a wonderful excuse to revisit the breathtaking wine country of Napa Valley. With help from our talented family—my sister Heather (co-photographer and marketing manager) and cousin Elaine (writer, editor, and source of never-ending information about the world of publishing)—this book was born.

During our visits and interviews, we quickly learned that winery dogs are inextricably connected to the culture, spirit, and essence of the wineries they call home. Unlike most other dogs, winery dogs go to work with people, day by day, at the wineries and in the vineyards, inside and outside, making guests happy and traipsing through the vines. With so much interaction between dogs and family members, employees, and guests, the connection these dogs have to the wineries takes on a special significance. As Jon Frazier of Frazier Winery told us, the right dog brings something spiritual to the whole operation. And at ninety-six wineries in Napa Valley, we saw this was true. Dogs bring out the best in people, and then people give their best selves to the wine. How can the winemaking process not be positively influenced by these loving dogs?

From tiny toy poodles to rottweilers and bullmastiffs, winery dogs come in all shapes and sizes. They arrive at wineries as puppies or adults. They come from breeders, friends, shelters, or newspaper ads. They are surprises on doorsteps, in garbage cans, or under bridges. They are shy or bold, mellow or full of energy. And in no time, whatever their size and origin and temperament, they fit right in.

Winery dogs are greeters, tasters, entertainers, herders, healers, protectors, hunters, chasers, celebrities, and sales enhancers. Older dogs train the new ones, bigger dogs protect the smaller ones, and all of them get on remarkably well with the winery cats. They ride in winery vehicles; they run beside employees in the fields; they sit nicely as visitors arrive for tastings. Better companions would be hard to find.

Immediately after publishing the first edition, we were overwhelmed with phone calls and e-mails. Winery owners all over Napa Valley told us their dogs would be perfect for the next book, and winery owners whose dogs were already featured told us about their new amazing puppies. It didn't take much convincing to see that we needed to make this expanded edition a truly new, exciting book. As before, our work in Napa Valley was a family adventure, this time with our new son, Andrew, coming along for the shoots and interviews. As we discovered, even the most energetic dogs in Napa would slow down to interact with our baby. Andrew was equally fascinated. Also in this edition, we added wine labels to our pages, discovering that the artistry and elegance of the labels created outstanding visual appeal.

To see and experience the gifts these dogs bring to the wineries was instantly rewarding for us, and every memory just compounds the good feeling. We would like to thank everyone we met at the wineries for the warm receptions, lively conversations, patience, encouragement, and delicious wine. The welcoming people of Napa Valley have made our project a journey we will always treasure. We hope that everyone who reads *Winery Dogs of Napa Valley* will experience the same affection and inspiration we felt at every winery we were privileged to visit.

Calistoga

Castello di Amorosa

Delectus Winery

Dutch Henry Winery

Envy Wines

Graeser Estate & Winery

Ramian Estate Vineyards

Vincent Arroyo Winery

Zahtila Vineyards

Diamond Mountain

CONSTANT—Diamond Mountain Vineyard & Winery

LUPO
CASTELLO DI AMOROSA

Despite the new winery's grandeur, Lupo—a seven-year-old German shepherd whose name means "wolf"—commands attention as he lies in a stately fashion at the tasting room's front door. Loyal, loving, and sensitive, Lupo is the perfect companion for winery owner Dario Sattui, and he's never far from him. He makes new friends every day, mingling expertly and winning the affection of every staff member, guest, and visiting dog. A star of his own making, Lupo will soon be featured on a poster so that guests can admire his striking looks even when he's roaming through the Cabernet Sauvignon vines or accompanying Dario on his travels.

2003
DOG IN STYLE
NAPA VALLEY
RED WINE

ALC. 15.1% BY VOL.

Fannie Mae

SPLASH & FANNIE MAE
DELECTUS WINERY

Fannie Mae, a six-year-old Border collie, sings to winery owner Linda Reisacher in the morning and stays close by her side day in and day out. When guests visit the tasting room, she greets them sweetly and then relaxes under the tasting room table. One-year-old Splash, an Australian shepherd with bloodlines of the family's former companion, Flash, clowns around and smiles frequently. To amuse himself, he rolls vigorously in the property's front bushes, unties guests' shoes, and tickles the feet of winemaker Gerhard Reisacher. When he's not pulling Fannie Mae's collar or trying to be a lap dog, he's napping hard—his nose on the ground and his tongue on the floor.

Sadie

Buggsy

Sissy

Henry

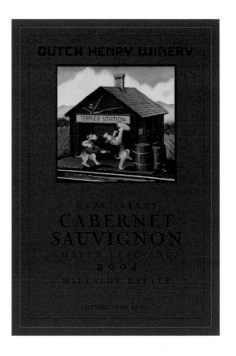

BUGGSY, SADIE, HENRY & SISSY
DUTCH HENRY WINERY

Weekday visitors to the Dutch Henry Winery are greeted by winemaker Scott Chafen's two vivacious Airedale terriers: Lady Buggsy of Blue Acre-Avalon, with distinctive white paws, and Avalon's Lady Pink Sadie, whose curvy tail can be seen wagging from a distance. Visitors who don't watch their bags may be surprised to see Sadie running off with their water bottles—Sadie loves toys, but she loves visitors' water bottles more. Weekend visitors are greeted not only by Buggsy and Sadie, but by winery owner Less Chafen's pugs, Henry and Sissy. During the week, Henry and Sissy work with Maggie Chafen at Dottie Dolittle, a children's clothing store in San Francisco, greeting customers and making children laugh. At Dutch Henry, away from the busy world of retail sales, they have more room to run around, but they still race to greet winery visitors, never tiring of being petted.

Winery Dogs of Napa Valley

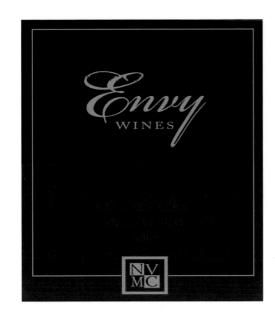

MOXIE
ENVY WINES

Moxie, a young Chihuahua, was born near Moxee, Washington. On her first day with Sherri Dobay, supertaster and designer, and Mark Carter, co-proprietor, Moxie visited five wineries in Walla Walla, proving herself a sound traveler. At home in the Napa Valley, she walks in the vineyard with Mark in the mornings, naps on the highest pillows in the afternoon, and barks from her bed at night to scare away the coyotes. In the tasting room, as guests sip Bee Bee's Blend, named for co-proprietor Nils Venge's best friend, Moxie is happy to show off her repertoire of tricks: crawling the carpet, sitting, speaking, singing, and spinning. Those who can't get enough of Moxie—a common occurrence—can find apparel designed with her image at www.moxiedog.com.

Jill

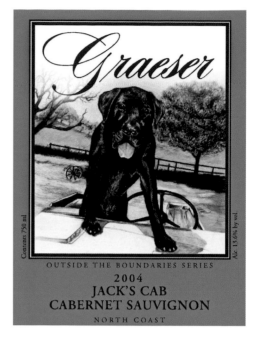

JACK & JILL
GRAESER ESTATE & WINERY

Jack, a five-year-old black Labrador retriever/Great Dane mix, and Jill, a sixteen-month-old Great Dane, are eager to greet approaching guests and lead them to the tasting room. There, as winery owner Richard Graeser explains the intricacies of wine appreciation and pours a variety of wines, the dogs collapse on the cool floor. As the guests move to the picnic areas, the dogs follow, endearing themselves and hoping that scraps will fall into their mouths. In the vineyards, Richard says the dogs "do more damage than deer," feasting for hours on grapes, ripe tomatoes, and fallen pears. Despite their appetite for destruction, Graeser recently released Jill's Juice Merlot, and will soon release Jack's Cab—two special additions to the popular "Outside the Boundaries" dog series.

WELCOME TO Graeser Winery

Jack

BAILEY
RAMIAN ESTATE VINEYARDS

When vineyard owner Brian Graham spotted Bailey, a Labrador retriever/Great Dane mix, at a shelter on Valentine's Day, he fell in love with him instantly. It was impossible to resist Bailey's constantly wagging tail, Brian says, which was—and still is—"thicker than a tree trunk." Today, at age seven, Bailey looks imposing but is truly always a sweet companion. All day long he runs through the Cabernet Sauvignon vineyards, returning sporadically to the front seat of Brian's truck for a few good naps.

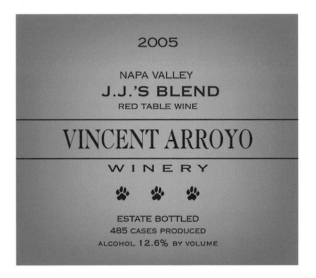

2005

NAPA VALLEY
J.J.'S BLEND
RED TABLE WINE

VINCENT ARROYO

W I N E R Y

🐾 🐾 🐾

ESTATE BOTTLED
485 CASES PRODUCED
ALCOHOL 12.6% BY VOLUME

Bodega

J.J. & BODEGA
VINCENT ARROYO WINERY

A customer gave J.J., now an eight-year-old black Labrador retriever, to winery owner and winemaker Vincent Arroyo. Like Joy, the Greenwood Ranch's previous black Labrador retriever, J.J. is an inspiration, an entertainer, and a wine connoisseur. In her best role, she inspires Vincent to create the red table wine he calls J.J.'s Blend. "You can't make wine without a dog," says Vincent. She is also a masterful entertainer, climbing on wine barrels to catch tennis balls that guests throw to her. In the evening, she unwinds with a glass of red wine poured over her lamb-and-rice dinner. Bodega, a two-year-old chocolate Labrador retriever, enjoys long visits to the winery when Adrian and Matt Moye, Vincent's daughter and son-in-law, come to work. Whenever Vincent drives the golf cart, Bodega chases him until he stops. Then she hops on, happy for the ride.

J.J.

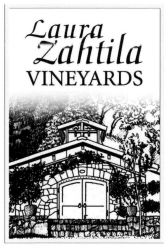

CALISTOGA,
NAPA VALLEY

Zinfandel

OAT HILL ESTATE

2005

ALC. 15.5% BY VOL.

ZOE
ZAHTILA VINEYARDS

Zoe, Laura Zahtila's gentle seven-year-old yellow Labrador retriever, is a natural at greeting visitors. It's no surprise that Zoe's mother, a yellow Labrador at RustRidge Ranch and Winery, is a renowned greeter as well. Zoe belonged at Zahtila right away—she laid her head on Laura's shoulder the moment they met, and Laura's nephews quickly named her. Today, Zoe not only greets the workers in the vineyard and tasting room, but she welcomes guests as their cars arrive at the winery. Lying on the front deck, sometimes in the sun and sometimes in the shade, she waits for the sound of tires on the gravel. Before the car is even parked, Zoe is waiting by the driver's door with a squeaky toy in her mouth, wagging her tail and hoping to be petted. She leads visitors to the tasting room and stays with them until they feel at home. Then she assumes her position on the deck, listening for the sound of the next approaching engine.

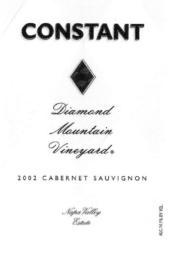

CONSTANT

Diamond Mountain Vineyard®

2002 CABERNET SAUVIGNON

Napa Valley Estate

ALC. 14.1% BY VOL

Caso

CASO & FLOOZY
CONSTANT–DIAMOND MOUNTAIN VINEYARD & WINERY

At CONSTANT–Diamond Mountain Winery, the two Portuguese water dogs take their jobs at the winery seriously. Caso de Vino, fourteen years old and recently blind, is director of tasting. When he begins eating the Cabernet Sauvignon grapes in the vineyard, winery owners Fred and Mary Constant know their grapes are ripe. Caso (which in Portuguese means "lover") was "awesome in his day," says Fred—no deer was safe in the vineyards when Caso was there. Caso's companion, the equally beautiful four-year-old Floozy Fairbanks, is the director of hospitality. At the sorting table, she monitors the sorting of grapes to be sure they're perfect, and with guests, she takes the lead to make sure they feel comfortable. When Fred takes visitors in his Swiss Army troop carrier on a 45-minute thrill ride through one of Napa's highest vineyards, Floozy—who is shameless about her love of affection, even in a bumpy vehicle—keeps the visitors from getting too nervous. Floozy and Caso both demonstrate their love of the land, as well as the stunning swimming pools, and visitors who watch them gracefully run and swim can't help but enjoy themselves, too.

Carneros

Acacia Vineyard

Bouchaine Vineyards

Buena Vista Carneros Winery

Ceja Vineyards

Etude Wines

Madonna Estate Winery

Saintsbury

Mt. Veeder

Hess Collection Vineyards

Jellybean

Riley

Roxy

JELLYBEAN, RILEY & ROXY
ACACIA VINEYARD

Jellybean, Riley, and Roxy are comical characters—each one an oddball. Jellybean, a nine-year-old mutt, loves to greet people "wearing her white shoes," says winery chef Kevin Simonson, referring to Jellybean's black legs and white paws. However, if someone has a ball in hand, she is powerless to do anything but stare at it, for hours, if need be, until it's in play. Riley, a six-year-old black Labrador retriever mix, is nicknamed "Jerry Rice" because of his ability to hone in on the ball and always make the catch, says Mike Beguelin, Acacia's official Man of Luxury and Leisure. Riley does his best to agitate Roxy, an eleven-year-old yellow Labrador retriever mix, but Roxy—a mellow presence and an agile swimmer—does her best to resist. Roxy has a keen sense of smell and spends hours sniffing the ground. In honor of their funny dogs, Acacia produces a limited quantity of a red table wine known as Mongrel Rouge.

MONGREL ROUGE

CALIFORNIA TABLE WINE
Undistinguished Pedigree & Uncertain Lineage

13% ALC BY VOLUME CONTAINS SULFITES
PRODUCED AND BOTTLED BY ACACIA WINERY, NAPA, CA

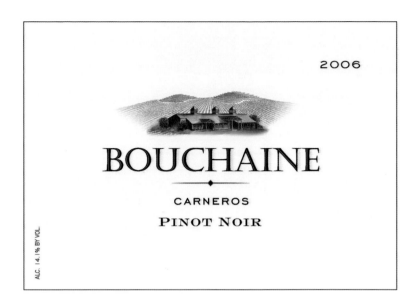

2006

BOUCHAINE

CARNEROS

PINOT NOIR

ALC. 14.1% BY VOL.

EARL
BOUCHAINE VINEYARDS

Earl, a mutt—possibly part rottweiler and part German shepherd—lives in the moment. Abandoned as a puppy on July 4 at Acacia Vineyard, he was quickly adopted by Bill Murray, a former Acacia employee who is now Bouchaine's associate winemaker. Earl walks to work on his own schedule and leaves by his own time clock. One day when an Oakland news reporter arrived at the vineyards, Earl suddenly leapt on the reporter's three-wheeler and accompanied him during the live filming. These days Earl darts out to join Bill, an avid marathoner, for a mile or two of running, exhibiting obvious pleasure in every step.

TRIXIE
BUENA VISTA CARNEROS WINERY

Trixie, a three-year-old Border collie, has one mission: to keep Charlie O'Brien in line. She loves to run through the vineyards, chase the rabbits, and torment the chickens and gophers, but she always races back to check on Charlie, the maintenance technician for all equipment inside the winery. She's extremely protective of him and his children. Even when there is no one staying at the winery's guest house, she circles through the yard to maintain her sphere of influence. Once, when Charlie left for a few days, she stayed with Charlie's friend Mike. Desperate to see what Charlie was up to, though, she dug a tunnel under Mike's property and ran at breakneck speed to find him. Charlie wonders if he'll ever get to go away again.

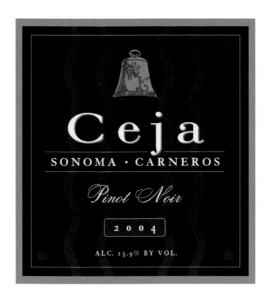

BRUJA
CEJA VINEYARDS

Bruja, an eleven-year-old Alaskan husky/Australian shepherd mix, is an essential part of the winery's hospitality team. Though *bruja* means "witch" in Spanish, it also carries the connotation of *curandera*, which means "healer." As vineyard owner Amelia Ceja says, "she really makes everyone around her feel better." Bruja warmly welcomes guests, understands both English and Spanish, and accompanies winemaker Armando Ceja on vineyard tours. When she's not with guests, Bruja chases rabbits from the vineyard, monitors the coming and going of other dogs, savors Pinot Noir grapes, and enjoys gourmet food. After a long day at work, she appreciates her favorite meal of grilled boneless and skinless chicken breasts marinated in olive oil, lime juice, garlic, and Spanish saffron.

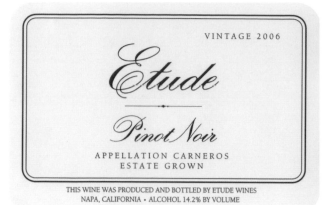

VINTAGE 2006

Etude

Pinot Noir

APPELLATION CARNEROS
ESTATE GROWN

THIS WINE WAS PRODUCED AND BOTTLED BY ETUDE WINES
NAPA, CALIFORNIA · ALCOHOL 14.2% BY VOLUME

Kelsea

KONA & KELSEA
ETUDE WINES

Kona, an eight-year-old chocolate Labrador retriever named for his beautiful coloring, once ate an entire cherry pie that viticulturist Franci Ashton had left on the counter. And while eating is still his favorite pastime, swimming is a close second, so he never refuses an opportunity to dive into the Napa River or one of the winery's reservoirs. A lovable friend, Kona is always happy to be petted. Kelsea, a six-year-old kelpie, is not as interested in eating as in working. As her sisters herd cattle at a farm, Kelsea herds bungs in Etude's cellar. On long-distance horse rides with winemaker and director of operations Jon Priest, she has the stamina to run 50 miles, cooling herself in puddles along the way and always making sure the horses stay on the trail. At home, after playing fetch with tennis balls, she curls up with her best friend, Toes, a calico cat.

Kelsea (left) &
Kona

Jake (left) &
Dodger

Winery Dogs of Napa Valley

Ellie May

ELLIE MAY, SHASTA, JAKE & DODGER
MADONNA ESTATE WINERY

The lucky dogs at Madonna Estate have the run of 160 acres of land and a duck-filled lake to plunge into. In addition, Ellie May, a twelve-year-old blue tick hound mix, takes care of all mole problems, swallowing them swiftly one at a time. Meanwhile, Shasta, a ten-year-old greyhound/afghan/wolf mix, tries to keep all the other dogs in line. Unfortunately for Shasta, Jake—an eight-year-old redbone hound/collie mix—has a mission to stir everyone up. Not taking the bait, Dodger, a four-year-old mutt, remains a tranquil companion who tolerates the costumes he wears on Halloween. Inside the Bartolucci family's home is a beautiful painted mural featuring happy wandering dogs, a true reflection of the dogs' lives outside.

Shasta

Champ

Carneros
PINOT NOIR
2005

SAINTSBURY

PRODUCED AND BOTTLED BY SAINTSBURY
NAPA, CALIFORNIA, USA   ALCOHOL 13.5% BY VOLUME

CHAMP & SCOUT
SAINTSBURY

Champ and Scout, both nine-year-old Border collies, were adopted from a cardboard box outside a Target in Vallejo. At the vineyards, both like to chase rabbits and balls for hours. At a winery-owned ranch on Henry Road, they herd the cattle, which involves a lot of barking, chasing, and rolling in cow patties. Sometimes they get so carried away that they herd the winery cats, Beau and Ralph, as well. "Champ and Scout keep us grounded and amused," say general manager David Graves and his wife, Elizabeth McKinney. "They're a constant source of comfort and companionship."

Scout

HESS
COLLECTION

**MOUNT VEEDER ~ NAPA VALLEY
CABERNET SAUVIGNON**

ESTATE GROWN

ROWDY
HESS COLLECTION VINEYARDS

If there were no vehicles at the vineyards, Rowdy—a three-year-old Catahoula hound from Ukiah—would run free all day, taking quick breaks to rest on the quiet, shady hills with the loveliest views. But once an ATV revs up, Rowdy runs as if he's at the races, chasing the tires as far as they go. Inside a truck, Rowdy desperately wants to drive; once he even took the wheel from Bob, a tractor mechanic, and now Bob knows to grip the wheel tightly and keep one eye on Rowdy. Bob hopes that one day Rowdy will find other interests. With luck, Rowdy will soon chase deer from the vineyards, settle down enough to be petted and admired, and leave the ATVs alone once in a while.

Napa County

Abruzzini Vineyards

Altamura Winery and Vineyards

Domaine La Due

Elkhorn Peak Cellars

Elyse Winery

Esser Vineyards

Frazier Winery

Kirkland Ranch Winery

Miss Olivia Brion Pinot Noir

Monticello Vineyards

Schrader Vineyards

Silenus Vintners

GRADY
ABRUZZINI VINEYARDS

Grady, a one-year-old yellow Labrador retriever, chases jackrabbits and cows and swims in the pond all day while Justin Sheaff, whose family owns the renowned vineyards, drives the tractor. After work, Grady catches his prized tennis balls thrown by Katie Chauncy, a Napa winery employee. He also demonstrates his strength by hefting large pieces of firewood from the fire pile. In the rare moments when he's not running, doing laps, fetching, or lifting, Grady quietly carries rocks in his mouth, wagging his tail. At home he lies very still as he sleeps, thoroughly worn out.

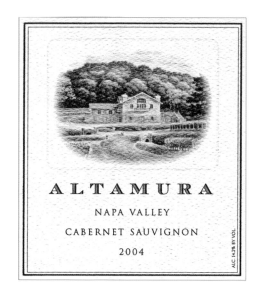

WOODY
ALTAMURA WINERY AND VINEYARDS

Woody, a nine-year-old Hovawart, is calm around visitors, lying at their feet and always ready to be petted. For the most part, he's very laid-back, choosing to drink red wine (for his heart), riding in the Jeep with winery owners Frank and Karen Altamura, or sleeping on the cave's cool floor. But big birds set him off. Woody spends hours chasing turkeys from the vineyards, and he tries in vain to catch egrets sitting placidly on the treetops. Sometimes buzzards circle above the property in large loops. Below them Woody circles, too, making sure they don't touch down.

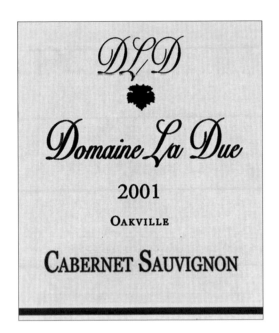

CHIANTI
DOMAINE LA DUE

Chianti, a six-year-old golden retriever, is a joyful best friend to winery owners Douglas and Angela Due. In the vineyards, Chianti loves to run free and to watch Angela's father, John Guman, on the tractor as it ambles past the vines at the base of Mt. George. At home alone on her favorite leather chair, she keeps watch over the neighborhood, but she's not a guard dog. "If a burglar came to the house," Angela jokes, "she would probably help him carry out the VCR." When Doug and Angela come home, Chianti—ready to burst with excitement—dances as they walk in the door. And when Doug sings, Chianti sings along, her beautiful brown eyes full of love for her family.

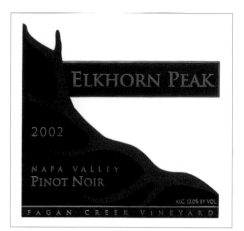

Cody

MAGGIE & CODY
ELKHORN PEAK CELLARS

Cody, an eight-year-old German shepherd, came from the pound as a puppy and impressed cofounder and grape-grower Ken Nerlove and his family right away. Smart and gracious, Cody could have been an excellent police or guide dog. When he was four, the family returned to the pound to find him a companion. While most of the dogs there were jumping and barking in their cages, one mutt—who shared a cage with a German shepherd—simply gazed at them, watching silently yet turning away whenever they looked at her. They left that day but couldn't stop thinking about the skinny, odd-looking dog who was so shy. When they brought her home, however, the eleven-month-old Maggie romped through the yard and dunked her entire head in the water bowl. Today, at age five, Maggie is still full of energy, leading Cody in her capers—stealing food in the kitchen and chasing the cat. The Nerlove family knows that while they are at work at the winery, the patient, calm Cody and the adventurous Maggie are perfect companions.

Maggie

Bubba

Elyse Winery

OTIS & BUBBA
ELYSE WINERY

Otis

Otis, a nine-year-old German shorthair, and Bubba, a five-year-old boxer, are teacher and student, respectively. When winemaker Mike Trotta began working with winery owners Ray and Nancy Coursen, he brought the puppy Bubba with him. Otis immediately found the perfect student and taught Bubba to point—and now the winery has two expert squirrel dogs. Otis also taught Bubba to keep pace with visitors to guide them to the tasting room. During harvest, Bubba learned the tasting techniques quickly. Like Ray, who continually searches for "the most wonderful fruit" for his wine, Otis and Bubba can't keep away from the best-tasting specimens. According to Nancy, the two easily eat their weight in grapes.

LUDWIG & MAX
ESSER VINEYARDS

Max

Max, a nine-year-old bullmastiff/Labrador retriever mix, has a huge physique as well as a huge heart. Full of affection for everyone, he is happy to wander the Esser property—a fresh egg from the chicken coop in his mouth—looking for someone to pet him. If he wanders too long, though, his friend Ludwig, a five-year-old dachshund, will pry the egg from Max's jaws and gobble it down. But Ludwig, named for King Ludwig of Bavaria, doesn't stay long. As the "chairman of the board," Ludwig is a busy dog, accompanying Manfred, Barbara, Sophie, and Julia as they make marketing calls, attend conferences, and play tennis. After a full day, he races back out to the chicken coop for another fresh egg, knowing that if Max is in his path, he'll get his egg a little sooner.

Ludwig

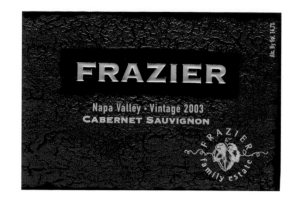

JET
FRAZIER WINERY

Jet, a ten-year-old golden retriever mix—fathered by an unknown black dog around the corner—is vineyard manager Jon Frazier's steadfast companion and morale booster. In the vineyards, Jet is crucial to keeping the workers' spirits high day by day, whether he's giving them affection or entertaining them with his antics. One day, as Jet chased a rabbit, the rabbit raced up a worker's body and used his head as a springboard, leaping away from Jet and making everyone laugh. Another day Jet somehow got into the adjacent golf course, and an amused golfer lifted Jet over the high fence to return him to Jon. Jet has also visited retirement communities, where the residents love to pet and feed him. "There's something spiritual about what Jet brings to us," Jon says. "On the most difficult days, this job would be terrible without my dog."

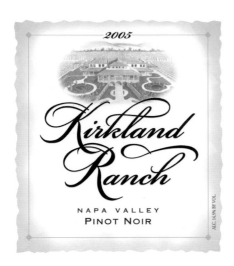

EDNA
KIRKLAND RANCH WINERY

Edna, a three-year-old Scottish terrier, is a model, greeter, stress reducer, and loving best friend. Posing expertly, Edna lends her gorgeous coloring and spark to winery photos and enhances the value of every product she stands beside. As a first-class greeter, she warmly welcomes everyone and pays extra attention to babies and older people who visit the tasting room. When stress hits the office, Edna races to the rescue, bringing joy to employees who need a quick break. After a long workday, she runs through the vineyard chasing butterflies, lizards, and groundhogs and then relaxes with her best friends—Debi Kirkland, director of administration, and the Kirkland Ranch cats.

MISS OLIVIA BRION
MISS OLIVIA BRION PINOT NOIR

Miss Olivia Brion, a five-year-old standard poodle, may be the only dog to have a wine named for her. A constant companion to David Mahaffey, winemaker and partner, she is with him every step of the artisanal winemaking process—whether he's tending the vineyard in the Wild Horse Valley, pressing grapes, moving barrels, or bottling his sought-after Pinot Noir. Miss Olivia, affectionately known as Libby, is an incredible athlete, chasing squirrels, wild turkeys, and deer and running in a big sine wave on the hillside alongside David as he bicycles for miles. Alison Mahaffey, David's daughter, is most impressed with Libby's sensitive nature. Not only does Olivia get along with other dogs and protect Flock, the family's chicken, but she senses when people are feeling bad and will gently lick their hands to show she understands.

JAKE
MONTICELLO VINEYARDS

Jake, an eight-year-old black Labrador retriever, spends his days wandering nonchalantly across Chris Corley's property. But as visitors find out, often too late, Jake is a master in the art of the hard sell. On tours, Jake greets visitors warmly and impresses them with his running speed and adept swimming. Then he charms them further by opening the doors to the winery. But once the guests enter the tasting room, Jake blocks the exit with his impressive weight, silently pressuring guests to make a purchase if they ever want him to move. As guests leave with their wine, Jake nuzzles up against them as if nothing ever happened.

Stoli (left) &
Bailey

2005
Cabernet Sauvignon
Napa Valley

SCHRADER
VINEYARDS

750ML   ALC 12.8% BY VOL

BAILEY & STOLI
SCHRADER VINEYARDS

Stoli

No one can miss the sights and sounds of Bailey and Stoli at Schrader Vineyards. Bailey, at two years old, is the official guard dog, racing from one post to another with a toy in her mouth. Stoli, the one-year-old fashionable adventurer, begins the day with a clean white coat and a longing to run through the vineyards. Within hours, her coat is lavender and her belly is full of Cabernet Sauvignon grapes. Both dogs accompany Danielle and Zachary Pacheco to tastings, marketing events, and getaways to see friends at Conn Creek, Mumm's, and Napa Valley Grille, where the chef creates special dog treats. All day long, the two French bulldogs snort so loudly they can be mistaken for pigs, and at night, their snores reverberate throughout the house.

Silenus Vintners
A Collection of Artisan Winemakers
"Silenus was the tutor & faithful companion to Dionysus, the Greek god of wine."

HANNAH
SILENUS VINTNERS

At her former home in Half Moon Bay, Hannah, an eleven-year-old golden retriever, used to be afraid of loud noises, even ceiling fans. But since her move to the winery with her family—Joni, Bob, and Ashlee Williamson—she is a new dog. Today she is happy to hang out by the forklifts or the other loud equipment, clearly enjoying the noise and endless activity around her. In the tasting room, she leans on guests to encourage constant petting, and in the barrel room, where wine tasting from the barrels is always going on, she laps up spilled wine. The winemakers also bring energetic dogs, a bonus for Hannah. Now that she lives in her ideal environment, she is happy to welcome all the visiting dogs and people and show them around.

Oakville

Gargiulo Vineyards

Groth Vineyards & Winery

Miner Family Vineyards

Oakville Ranch Vineyards

Plumpjack Winery

Rudd Vineyards & Winery

Saddleback Cellars

Turnbull Wine Cellars

GARGIULO VINEYARDS
ESTATE GROWN
OAKVILLE, NAPA VALLEY

LILY
GARGIULO VINEYARDS

Inspecting gardens is an arduous task, as Lily—the nine-year-old Maltese—knows well. She carefully examines each garden, nosing her way between bushes and sniffing every flower and herb, and she chases gophers down into their holes. Only the sound of tires on the gravel driveway can set her running to the winery. Visitors fall in love with her immediately and threaten to steal her on the way out. Some guests even send her home-baked treats and handmade clothes. But as soon as the guests leave—without Lily, as the Gargiulo family ensures—she hurries back to the gardens. By the end of the day, her white hair is filled with rosemary, sage, and vineyard dust.

China Moon

CHINA MOON &
CHOU MEI MEI
GROTH VINEYARDS & WINERY

Chou Mei Mei

China Moon and Chou Mei Mei, ages sixteen and two, are such striking dogs that nobody can ignore them at the winery. The bold pugs, together with sixteen-year-old Frank Fat and six-month-old Moo Shoo (not pictured), have created havoc by snatching toys, pacifiers, and food from small children—and they've even chewed on tasters' beautiful sandals at the bar. Away from the crowd, China Moon takes no guff from Chou Mei Mei (whose name means "little sister" in Mandarin), especially when the younger pug takes China's beloved Audubon mallard toy or tries to commandeer Dennis Groth's lap. Luckily, Chou Mei Mei never sulks, finding other noisy bird toys or catching bits of food flying from Genevieve Groth's high chair. "Pugs have a great sense of humor," says Judy Groth, "and they amuse us all day long."

Chou Mei Mei

Ella

ELLA & BESSY
MINER FAMILY VINEYARDS

Ella, an eight-year-old springer spaniel, is an office dog most days. She loves customers, other dogs, and even cats, and she chases lizards in the vineyards for hours. To Dave Miner's dismay, however, she has to be kept away from picnickers. A shameless beggar, she once snuck away from an employee barbeque with a large rib in her mouth—stolen from an employee's plate. So it was no wonder that she started putting on weight. Luckily, Bessy, a two-year-old springer spaniel, came on the scene. Constantly in motion, Bessy is forever hunting for balls in the vineyards and bushes. And because Ella feels the need to look after Bessy's every move, Ella runs around all day, too, missing out on any unattended plates of food.

Bessy

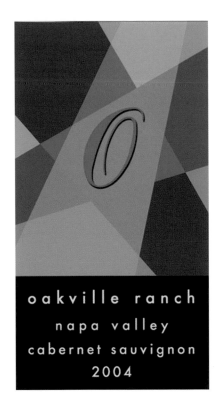

oakville ranch
napa valley
cabernet sauvignon
2004

ROMEO
OAKVILLE RANCH VINEYARDS

Romeo, a six-year-old bull mastiff, has proved he can be as dramatic as his Shakespearean namesake. A fine greeter and "ambassadog," Romeo loves to watch a particular cat that lingers on the property. One day he ventured to the cat's favorite part of the vineyards. To the horror of general manager Paula Kornell, he came back dragging the back half of his body—convincing her he'd been attacked by a snake. Upon closer inspection, however, it was clear that Romeo had simply suffered a minor cat scratch and was hoping for some excitement and sympathy.

Hallie

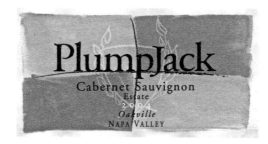

HALLIE & REGGIE
PLUMPJACK WINERY

Hallie and Reggie know how to please a crowd. Hallie, an eight–year-old English springer spaniel, is so popular that John Conover, the winery's general manager, gets frequent letters and e-mails from starstruck visitors asking about her. Reggie, also known as Sir Reginald's Rip Tide, is a four-year-old black Labrador retriever with a similar gift of celebrity. As winemaker Tony Biagi says, Reggie is known as the resident "rock star" because visitors get excited when he's around. Fortunately, Hallie and Reggie both know how to take a break from their admirers. Hallie eats Cabernet Sauvignon grapes until she's full, finds a nice spot in the sun for napping, and grins—John says—as the grapes ferment in her stomach. Reggie cools down in the pond, swimming quietly in his solitude until he hears the call of the winery's restless crowd.

Reggie

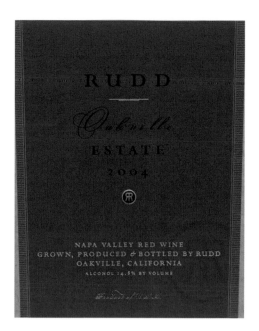

RUDD

Oakville

ESTATE

2004

ℝ

NAPA VALLEY RED WINE
GROWN, PRODUCED & BOTTLED BY RUDD
OAKVILLE, CALIFORNIA
ALCOHOL 14.8% BY VOLUME

TESS
RUDD VINEYARDS & WINERY

Tess, a five-year-old Bernese mountain dog, is the winery's official greeter. When winery owner Leslie Rudd arrives at the office each day, Tess is beside him. At the hospitality office, she receives her first biscuit of the day from her own cookie jar, and then she greets the staff one by one. Without fail, she finds her place at the front door to welcome every visitor. "Tess makes the entire experience here at Rudd feel approachable," says winery owner Susan Rudd. "Since Tess is such a gentle, friendly, and easygoing creature, she lets guests know immediately that they are welcome."

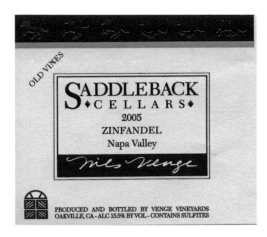

SCARLETT
SADDLEBACK CELLARS

Scarlett, an eight-year-old Cavalier King Charles Spaniel, is Saddleback's romantic starlet. Whenever Scarlett's Rose—the wine named for her—is brought out for tasting, she comes to life, entertaining guests with her beauty, gentleness, and charisma. Winery owner and winemaker Nils Venge says that although Scarlett enchants everyone, her excellent manners seem to "fly right out the door" as she runs through the vineyards to the Fleury residence and showers her boyfriend, Bailey, with puppy kisses.

TURNBULL

2005

Cabernet
Sauvignon

Estate Grown

Napa Valley

ALC. 14.5% BY VOL.

SODA
TURNBULL WINE CELLARS

Because winery owners Brigitte and Patrick O'Dell travel frequently to promote their Bordeaux varietals, they wanted a dog who would enjoy accompanying them. Soda, a one-year-old Westie, is their dream come true. On the plane and about town, she is content to rest in Brigitte's cashmere bag. At the winery and guesthouse, Soda is social and spry, happy to be petted by everyone. At home, she is entranced by most shows on Animal Planet and can watch a full-length movie with interest. But it is on the Turnbull grounds that she is truly in her element—sniffing, hunting, and leaping from bush to bush. The only trouble with Soda is that once she's outside, she never wants to leave. When Brigitte starts walking back home, Soda tugs at Brigitte's boot again and again, imploring her to stay just a little longer, for just a few more sniffs.

TURNBULL
WINE CELLARS

Rutherford

Fleury Estate Winery

Grgich Hills Cellar

Honig Vineyard & Winery

Long Meadow Ranch Winery

Provenance Vineyards

Quintessa

Rubicon Estate

Sequoia Grove Vineyards and Winery

Staglin Family Vineyard

Sullivan Vineyards

Swanson Vineyards

The Terraces

Trahan Winery

Riley (left) &
Bailey

FLEURY
ESTATE WINERY
NAPA VALLEY

RILEY & BAILEY
FLEURY ESTATE WINERY

Stepbrothers Riley and Bailey have always gotten along famously. Riley, a four-year-old Shih Tzu, immediately welcomed Bailey—a 4-year-old Teddy bear mix of Shih Tzu, bichon frise, and Yorkshire terrier—to the estate. Early each morning the pair walks companionably among the eleven acres of vineyards in Rutherford, taking time to sniff the landmark windmill, with winery owners Brian and Claudia Fleury. Inside and outside the vineyards, the dogs eat whatever interesting plant or insect they find, and then they lie around the rest of the day in the boutique winery's lovely tasting room, crunching on fallen breadsticks as guests sip Cabernet Sauvignon.

POSIP
GRGICH HILLS CELLAR

Posip, a nine-year-old Australian shepherd/Border collie mix, was named for the white wine that owner and winemaker Mike Grgich makes in Croatia. Maryanne Wedner, Mike's longtime assistant, picked Posip from her hairstylist's dog's litter to give Mike the perfect canine companion. Posip loved Mike right away, understanding his English and Croatian commands in no time. Today, after running freely in the vineyards, Posip greets visitors in the parking lot and licks their hands in the tasting room—instantly infusing happiness even before the guests taste the wine.

Raisin

Annie

BUZZ, ANNIE & RAISIN
HONIG VINEYARD & WINERY

Buzz

At Honig, a dog-friendly winery, employees can bring dogs with them for an exciting day. Whether in the tasting room, on the patio, or in a plastic kiddie pool, the dogs are always in motion. Annie, a six-year-old black Labrador retriever, is motivated by food inside or outside but is never far from office manager Patti Hawker, who only recently adopted her. Buzz, a three-year-old yellow Labrador retriever, loves to entertain visiting children when he's not exploring the grounds with sales and development manager Steven Honig and his children, Annika and Gavin. Raisin, a ten-month-old yellow Labrador retriever, often greets the winery's president, Michael Honig, and his wife, Stephanie, with a leaf in her mouth and a strong desire to play. After the winery closes, several employees take a daily three-mile loop through the scenic vineyards, inviting all the happy dogs to join them.

LILY
LONG MEADOW RANCH WINERY

Long Meadow Ranch may be the best place on earth for a social, food-loving golden retriever. At age eight, Lily delights in her routine. After breakfast, she walks with winery owner Laddie Hall all over the property, greeting the chickens, sniffing the red wattle pigs, and nuzzling the horses—Chief, Pokey, and Boo. Lily often indulges in a furtive snack of manure or horse hoof trimmings, and she loves leaping into swampy ponds and rolling in any smelly piece of earth she can find. After a hike in the woods, a bath, and some good brushing, she's thrilled to meet guests in the tasting room. Thanks to a memorable taste of a guest chef's Italian cooking, Lily is affectionately known as "Meatball" and is eager to munch on cheese, breadsticks, and carpaccio as the guests sip organic Cabernet Sauvignon. At night she sleeps at the foot of the bed, barking whenever she hears a vehicle pull up to her ranch.

Rowdy

GYPSY & ROWDY
PROVENANCE VINEYARDS

Gypsy Rain Rutherford Dust, a three-year-old toy poodle, sleeps with one eye open, waiting to dance at the sight of a new face. When it's time to play, Gypsy bounces down the stairs like a ballerina, silently springing across the smooth floor of the tasting room and weaving in and out of the assemblage of legs, handbags, and any hand reaching down to pet her. "Gypsy has a way of softening everyone's mood," say winemaker Tom Rinaldi and his daughter Angelina. "She lifts our spirits and adds joy and motivation, especially on Mondays!" Rowdy, a four-month-old Australian shepherd, loves going to the vineyards with grower relations manager Elizabeth Florence-Forster. As soon as another dog is in sight, Rowdy crouches down in attack mode, fakes an attack, and then runs, inciting a wild chase.

Gypsy

SAMMY
QUINTESSA

Sammy, a nine-year-old mutt (possibly part Labrador retriever and part Dalmatian), came to winemaker Aaron Pott from a life spent indoors with a Hollywood director. Though the director said that Sammy hated water, the first thing Sammy did at the biodynamic vineyard was leap joyfully into the irrigation lake. At the sorting table, Sammy eats not only the rejected grapes but also the yellow jackets that bother everyone. Inside the tasting room, he'll put his head on any taster's lap in a plea for cheese, something he can't get enough of. When he sits, Sammy looks like a "sausage with four toothpicks," Aaron says, but when he runs, he looks positively heroic. When Nicolas Joly, the French ersatz patron saint of biodynamics, first saw Sammy running with abandon through the vineyard, he exclaimed, *"That dog is biodynamique!"*

Bodie

JACKIE BROWN, BRUNELLA & BODIE
RUBICON ESTATE

Brunella

When chief executive officer Jay Shoemaker first met Jackie Brown, a Chihuahua/terrier mix, at Pet Pride Day in Golden Gate Park, she licked his cheek. Later, when shelter volunteers brought her to his home, she ran up to him and bit his leg. Undaunted, Jay and his wife adopted her, and today, at age seven, she's a loving companion—enraptured by the refrigerator at home and calm in Jay's lap at work. Brunella, a four-year-old Italian spinone, struts like a supermodel and dives for rabbits through thick brambles, never getting scratched. International sales manager Heather de Savoye, in a nod to Bru's heritage, pours olive oil and grates Parmesan cheese on her dry food every day. Bodie, a twelve-week-old blue heeler, runs each morning on the expansive Rubicon estate, pausing occasionally to play with other dogs or roll over and let admiring women pet him. When Kelly McCown, executive chef, brings him to the beach, he's content to dig in the sand and play with sticks for hours, never wanting to go home.

GROWN, PRODUCED & BOTTLED ON THE ESTATE

Rubicon Estate

Rubicon

RUTHERFORD · NAPA VALLEY

2004

Jackie Brown

Daisy May

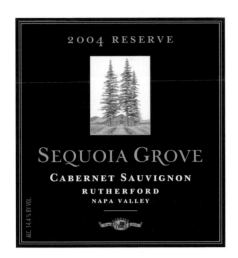

Sophie

SOPHIE & DAISY MAY
SEQUOIA GROVE VINEYARDS
AND WINERY

Sophie, an eleven-year-old rescue bulldog mix known as "Miss Waddle Butt," is loving, curious, and always concerned with keeping the staff and other dogs in order. Daisy May, a one-year-old French bulldog, is the winery's social butterfly. In fact, at her first winery party, despite the delicious Cabernet Sauvignon, she was the hit of the event. Every day on the estate, the two bulldogs run and play in the beautiful gardens, taking breaks to greet guests beneath the towering sequoias. At the end of the day, Ron Davidson, the director of hospitality, often takes an energetic walk in the vineyards— with Sophie and Daisy May just ahead of him, enjoying the fresh air and lively companionship.

STAGLIN
FAMILY VINEYARD
ESTATE
CABERNET SAUVIGNON
RUTHERFORD, NAPA VALLEY
2004
ESTATE BOTTLED BY STAGLIN FAMILY VINEYARD, RUTHERFORD, CA   750 ML   ALC. 14.9% BY VOL.
"WINGED WOMAN WALKING" SCULPTURE BY STEPHEN DE STAEBLER

KARA
STAGLIN FAMILY VINEYARD

Garen and Shari Staglin have traditionally had Jack Russell terriers at their winery. The Staglins' driveway is even flanked by two pillars featuring Jack Russell terriers on top. Two of their Jack Russells, Deuce and Sami, entertained cast and crew at the filming of Disney's 1997 remake of *The Parent Trap*, a film that featured the Staglins' villa and vineyards in many scenes. When coyotes became a problem at the vineyard, Garen and Shari got Kara, now a four-year-old Anatolian shepherd, as a guard dog. Each morning and late each afternoon, Kara surveys the vineyard on her walks with the Staglins. When she sees rabbits, turkeys, or deer, she darts off into the rows to chase them from the fruit. Between her patrols, she wades contentedly in the long, beautiful pool or rests in her own corral under a big oak tree. A loyal companion with a spirit of independence and a love of the land, Kara is clearly thriving at the Staglin home.

Apollo

Zsa Zsa

APOLLO, ZSA ZSA & BOE
SULLIVAN VINEYARDS

"**B**alls just fall from the sky at Sullivan Vineyards," says Kelleen Sullivan. Zsa Zsa, an eight-year-old golden retriever, and Boe, a seventeen-year-old yellow Labrador retriever, can't keep away from the Ball Tree, a prolific apple tree that seems to produce endless "balls" for them to pluck and carry to anyone who will throw them in a game of fetch. To Apollo, a two-year-old yellow Labrador retriever, nothing is better than a big stick. Every morning as he rides in the truck, he can hardly sit still, so Sean Sullivan lets him out at the end of the driveway and watches Apollo race to the vineyards. When he's not carrying his stick of the day, he's snacking on grapes, figs, and—if Zsa Zsa and Boe aren't watching—apples. Back at home, Sean's mother, Joanna, gives him big bones to tide him over until he can find his next big stick in the morning.

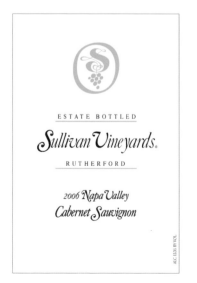

ESTATE BOTTLED

Sullivan Vineyards.

RUTHERFORD

2006 Napa Valley
Cabernet Sauvignon

Boe

Jack (left), Rufus
& Pinta

SWANSON
VINEYARDS
OAKVILLE
NAPA VALLEY

2005
MERLOT

Rufus

PINTA, JACK & RUFUS
SWANSON VINEYARDS

Pinta, a twelve-year-old terrier mix and loving companion to Clarke and Elizabeth Swanson, hangs out in a quiet corner of the office and shrewdly watches as her canine companions play with squeaker toys and interact with staff members. Jack, a mellow four-year-old black Labrador retriever, is content to snooze beside the Swansons' assistant Gail Alexander when he's not running across the backyard lawn or lying in the sun with three-year-old Rufus, a Norwich terrier with a big personality. As the Swansons have learned, Rufus is sweet and gentle, yet his bark is known to some as a "supersonic weapon"—piercing enough to break Coke bottles, or just get the attention he requires. As different as they can be, Pinta, Jack, and Rufus give everyone big doses of affection and much-needed comic relief on the busiest of days.

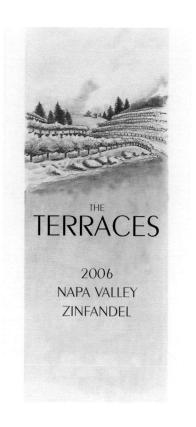

THE
TERRACES

2006
NAPA VALLEY
ZINFANDEL

Curry (left) &
Bella

CURRY & BELLA
THE TERRACES

very morning, Curry—a two-year-old yellow Labrador retriever—licks the face of winery owner Timm Crull to get him out of bed. Together they hit the vineyards, meeting up with Nate Page, assistant winemaker, and Bella, a one-year-old black Labrador retriever. For hours the dogs run through the Cabernet Sauvignon and century-old Zinfandel vines, barking at deer and snacking on figs and blood oranges. After napping in the shade on the cushioned seats of the Kawasaki Mules, Curry and Bella mingle with admirers on the guesthouse deck and within the four walls of the original winery, which was built in 1885 not far from an old rock quarry. Today the historic winery is the scene of festive celebrations illuminated by carnival lights and energized by interesting echoes and The Terraces' two happy Labs.

2006 Cameros
Pinot Noir

SADIE
TRAHAN WINERY

When winemaker Chuck Custodio and his wife, Janna, stopped by the pound one day, they asked which dog was the next to be put down. Next in line was Sadie, a six-year-old German shorthaired pointer who was picked up off the street with no collar and a tennis ball in her mouth. According to Chuck, in the last five years she hasn't dropped the ball since. When guests with children visit the winery, Sadie gives them a relaxing experience. The parents can take their time to drink wine while their kids throw the ball (or wine barrel bung) for Sadie, as far and as often as they can, laughing as they watch the "crazy running dog" go after it. A fiercely dependable presence, Sadie is the Cal Ripken, Jr. of the winery business, bringing happiness to everyone she sees every day.

Spring Mountain

Behrens & Hitchcock

Cain Vineyard & Winery

Domaine Charbay Winery & Distillery

Guilliams Vineyards

Juslyn Vineyards

Paloma Vineyard

Robert Keenan Winery

Schweiger Vineyards

Stony Hill Vineyard

Vineyard 7 & 8

Howell Mountain

Outpost Estate Wines

Venge Vineyards

Chien Lunatique

LUCY
BEHRENS & HITCHCOCK

Lucy, a nine-year-old Jack Russell terrier, is a daring individualist. At a young age, she was hit by a Ford 150, an ATV, and a motorcycle. When her pelvis was broken, she surprised everyone with her strong recovery. Today no one would know that she almost didn't make it. Though Jack Russell terriers are known for disliking water, Lucy spends countless hours at home splashing around in the swimming pool. Equally vivacious at work, she opens the heavy wooden winery doors with her teeth—evidenced by the bite marks in the wood—to chase lizards and mice in the vineyards. Winery owners Les Behrens and Lisa Drinkward, in awe of Lucy's energy and tenacity, have named a Syrah for her, Chien Lunatique.

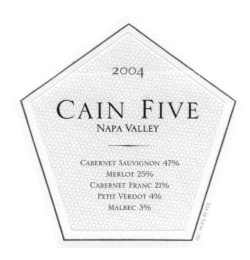

2004

CAIN FIVE
NAPA VALLEY

CABERNET SAUVIGNON 47%
MERLOT 25%
CABERNET FRANC 21%
PETIT VERDOT 4%
MALBEC 3%

ROBO
CAIN VINEYARD & WINERY

Robo, a seven-year-old rottweiler mix, is a true vineyard dog. With no single owner, he belongs to the vineyard crew, riding in the back of the pickup truck and bathing in the strong sunlight above the fog on Spring Mountain. He barely lifts his head when a rabbit hops by, and he tires out quickly when pursuing a deer. Instead, he prefers the camaraderie of the crew—and the burritos they share with him. Sometimes it seems Robo forgets he's a dog. One day, vineyard supervisor Gustavo De Haro led Robo to the garage to feed him. As Gustavo lifted the bag of dog food, a mouse ran out. One of Gustavo's colleagues in the barn screamed and jumped up on the counter. Robo, equally upset, ran outside and jumped up on the picnic table. Gustavo couldn't stop laughing at the gigantic dog who was afraid of such a tiny mouse.

Snifter

SUNNY & SNIFTER
DOMAINE CHARBAY WINERY & DISTILLERY

Sunny

Sunny and Snifter love to be near people—greeting them, walking alongside them, and making them happy. Sunny, an eight–year-old Australian shepherd/tick coonhound mix, runs to welcome visitors and kiss them over and over. Snifter, also known as "Sniffy," is a four-year-old Jack Russell terrier who pokes his nose into guests' cars to get a whiff—and maybe a taste—of their delicious snacks and pastries. As much as they love every visitor, they are most attached to Susan and Miles Karakasevic. At the end of the day, they lead the winery owners home, pausing at the gardens as Susan and Miles pick tomatoes for dinner. At home, Sunny settles down comfortably while Snifter falls deeply asleep on Miles' lap.

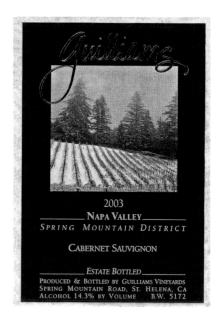

2003
NAPA VALLEY
SPRING MOUNTAIN DISTRICT

CABERNET SAUVIGNON

ESTATE BOTTLED
PRODUCED & BOTTLED BY GUILLIAMS VINEYARDS
SPRING MOUNTAIN ROAD, ST. HELENA, CA
ALCOHOL 14.3% BY VOLUME   B.W. 5172

ANGIE
GUILLIAMS VINEYARDS

Angie, an eleven-year-old black Labrador retriever, sleeps for much of the day in the azalea bushes, getting up occasionally to roll in the dirt or snow. At night she hunts in the vineyards, catching moles and getting sprayed by skunks. But her goal is clearly to meet a fox. Litters of foxes are born in the drain system, and workers can see the kits leaping up into the air and down into their holes by day. At night the foxes' cries can be heard a quarter of a mile away, and the sounds of their scurrying echo in the pipes. Angie waits for hours at different pipe openings, alert for the moment a fox will appear. As far as owner and winemaker John Guilliams knows, Angie has yet to see a fox. But as long as she wants to lie at the pipe openings at night, she'll always have a restful place to sleep in the day.

Charlie (left),
Luca & Nessie

NESSIE, TILLIE, LUCA, CHARLIE & JIMMY CHOO
JUSLYN VINEYARDS

When winery owner Carolyn Butler comes home, she's greeted by five gorgeous, happy dogs: Nessie, a seven-year-old papillon; Tillie, a seven-year-old tri-papillon; Luca, a three-year-old long-haired miniature dachshund; Jimmy Choo, a two-year-old papillon; and Charlie, a fifteen-week-old King Charles spaniel. In the mornings, the group runs between the rows of Cabernet Sauvignon vines, chasing quail and hares twice their size. Back at home, they bark whenever cars pull up in the driveway, but as soon as guests come inside, they perk up and play. Good-natured and sociable, they circulate with ease among family, friends, and celebrities at festive winery events.

Tillie

Jimmy Choo

AUSSIE
PALOMA VINEYARD

I n her younger years, Aussie—an Australian terrier—chased snakes and mice from the vines
as winery owners Barbara and Jim Richards cultivated Merlot and Syrah grapes on Spring
Mountain. When Aussie needed a break, Jim was always happy to let her hop on the ATV for
a ride. Today, at age fifteen, she spends most of her days relaxing in bed, strolling around the
house, and attending to her lifelong passion, eating. Graceful and affectionate in her retirement
years, she lounges each evening in the Richards' bedroom, always the faithful companion.

Keenan

K

2004
Cabernet Sauvignon
Napa Valley
SPRING MOUNTAIN DISTRICT
ESTATE BOTTLED BY ROBERT KEENAN WINERY
SPRING MOUNTAIN RD., SAINT HELENA, CALIFORNIA
ALCOHOL 14.3% BY VOLUME

SCOOBY & SCRAPPY
ROBERT KEENAN WINERY

Scrappy, a three-year-old black Labrador retriever mix, is a "big ham," says Laura Kewell, tasting-room manager and special-events coordinator. He loves attention, and he knows that visitors can't resist him when he runs to the parking lot to meet them. After leading them into the cool, dark tasting room, he tries hard to lie against everyone's feet at the bar. A true "mama's dog," he doesn't like to venture off alone. If Laura leads him down into the cellar of French and American oak barrels, he'll pull the barrel chalks and chew on them contentedly. Scooby, a twelve-year-old mutt who does not have Scrappy's social graces, tends to bark genially at visitors rather than greet them. But he has no trouble finding happiness any day of the week. He snacks on dried figs scattered on the property, rides with abandon on the work truck, and to the entertainment of anyone watching, slides down the winery's grassy hill on his back, over and over again, until he's hungry for more figs.

Scrappy (left) & Scooby

Sydney

Blitzen

SYDNEY, BLITZEN & TUCKER
SCHWEIGER VINEYARDS

Tucker, a ten-year-old yellow Labrador retriever, is a tranquil companion for winemaker Andrew Schweiger. While he enjoys tasting grapes outside, he prefers to lie indoors by the fire near any human or canine. Sydney, an eight-year-old yellow Labrador retriever, and her five-year-old daughter Blitzen—fathered by a stealthy Border collie named X—lead a carefree life. While Sydney greets visitors with a leaf, stick, or fir cone in her mouth, Blitzen shows off by bouncing a beach ball from her nose. Sydney tastes the ripe grapes, Blitzen follows winery owner Fred Schweiger everywhere, and at the end of the day they both enjoy resting beside the fire with Tucker.

SCHWEIGER
VINEYARDS
EST. 1982

2003
CABERNET SAUVIGNON
SPRING MOUNTAIN DISTRICT
NAPA VALLEY
ESTATE BOTTLED

Tucker

STONY HILL

NAPA VALLEY

CHARDONNAY

2005

Grown, produced and bottled 600 feet
above the floor of the Napa Valley by
Stony Hill Vineyard, St. Helena, CA

ALCOHOL 13% BY VOLUME CONTAINS SULFITES

Katie Scarlet

KATIE SCARLET & LUCIANO
STONY HILL VINEYARD

Luciano, a seven-year-old yellow Labrador retriever, was named after the bloodthirsty gangster "Lucky" Luciano. Fortunately, Luciano the Lab is mellow, calmly vacuuming Chardonnay grapes from the ground when employees are crushing. Longtime winemaker Mike Chelini, who loves all things Italian, still thinks the name fits—especially when he asks, in a heavy Italian accent, "Hey, Luch, how 'bout a glass of wine?" Luciano usually defers, preferring instead to follow Mike wherever he goes, even if Mike is speeding away on his Honda Foreman. Katie Scarlet, a gentle ten-year-old Brittany spaniel, was named after Scarlet O'Hara. Unlike the fictional character, though, Katie Scarlet—whose father was a champion show dog—is shy with strangers and doesn't care for men. With her excellent nose, she sniffs for hours alone in the vineyard, enjoying the quiet open spaces. She rests under proprietor Willenda McCrea's desk, a soothing, heartfelt companion and a peaceful presence.

Luciano

Yorki (left) &
Mel

SPRING MOUNTAIN DISTRICT

VINEYARD

7 & 8

NAPA VALLEY

MEL & YORKI
VINEYARD 7&8

Vineyard 7&8, a small family-run winery on the top of Spring Mountain, is the ultimate playground for two lucky dogs. Mel, a three-year-old golden retriever, longs to go to the winery as soon as winery manager and assistant winemaker Wesley Steffens says the word *work*. As Mel runs for her Frisbee, she also frantically nudges Wesley toward the car. Yorki, a seven-year-old black Labrador retriever, is what Alissa Flynn, the direct sales and hospitality manager, calls a "high-energy runner." When Mel and Yorki meet up at the winery, at last, no one can stop them. All day the two run through the vineyards, swim in the pond, and frolic in the enticing field of alfalfa—a lush, green piece of dog heaven filled with what Wes and his wife, Jess, believe is "canine catnip."

TEDDY & ELLIE
OUTPOST ESTATE WINES

Teddy and Ellie, one-year-old English mastiffs named for Theodore and Eleanor Roosevelt, are usually docile and low-key. At the winery, they gently greet visitors, and in the vineyards, they coolly chase the deer from the Zinfandel vines and stay close to winery owners Frank and Kathy Dotzler. When it's time for a break, they swim in the pond and relax on the hills, chewing each other's ears. Recently, however, the Dotzlers learned that Teddy—like his namesake—has a wild streak. For reasons even the Rough Riders would not have understood, Teddy thoroughly destroyed a down pillow, sending the feathers flying onto and under every piece of furniture in the room. Ellie, who is afraid to venture upstairs in the dark, has not yet unleashed her potential as an interior decorator.

Ellie (front) & Teddy

Lucy

Lucy (left) &
Sadie

LUCY & SADIE
VENGE VINEYARDS

Lucy, age three, and Sadie, age two, greet each other every morning on the winery's bridge and spend hours tugging on sticks or looking for cheese plates meant for the guests. Lucy was only seven weeks old when a rattlesnake bit her, but today the happy golden retriever is an accomplished entertainer, making guests smile as she guides them on tours alongside winery owners Nils and Kirk Venge. Her stage presence only intensifies when three creative girls at the winery dress her as a ballerina. While Lucy dances in the tasting room, Sadie–a beautiful boxer–runs like a bullet through the vineyards. When she needs a rest, Sadie relaxes in her comfortable bed in the lab beside her best friend, assistant winemaker Nick Briggs.

St. Helena

Anomaly Vineyards

Benessere Vineyards

Beringer Vineyards

Bremer Family Winery

Buehler Vineyards

Chappellet Vineyard & Winery

Chateau Boswell Winery

Clark - Claudon Vineyards

Corison Winery

Ehlers Estate

HALL Winery

Kelham Vineyards

Kuleto Estate Family Vineyards

Livingston Moffett Winery

Merryvale Vineyards

Parry Cellars

Raymond Vineyards

Rombauer Vineyards

RustRidge Ranch and Winery

Salvestrin Estate Vineyard and Winery

S.E. Chase Family Cellars

Spottswoode Estate Vineyard & Winery

V. Sattui Winery

Varozza Vineyards

Whitehall Lane Winery

ASHBY, COSETTE & DANNY
ANOMALY VINEYARDS

Thanks to winery owners Linda and Steve Goldfarb, Anomaly Vineyards is never without the love of a good dog. Years ago, the winery was ruled by Indee, a loving husky/shepherd mix whose image is on Anomaly's label. Today, in Indee's Vineyard, an eleven-year-old Jack Russell terrier mix named Ashby shares the run of the property with an older poodle mix, Cosette, and a one-year-old miniature poodle, Danny. As a puppy, Ashby was lucky that Linda happened to be driving by him at the right time. At the side of the road a woman was holding Ashby in the air, waving him around to attract attention. The Goldfarbs didn't need a new dog, but Ashby's leg was badly fractured and Linda knew the puppy needed a chance. Today Ashby is healthy and happy. Cosette, who was rescued on the streets of St. Helena, is his best friend, keeping an eye on him every day. Danny, the newest rescue dog at Anomaly, is a natural dancer, hopping and gliding with his unusually long legs. His favorite toy is Ashby's tail, and even though he hangs on it whenever he can, he doesn't seem to know why it keeps wagging and moving away from him.

Danny

Cosette

Ashby

STORMY
BENESSERE VINEYARDS

Benessere, a winery specializing in Italian varietals grown in the Napa Valley, was named for the Italian word that means "prosperity" and "well-being." Stormy, a ten-year-old Newfoundland, is the picture of health and the first to greet visitors each day. A prize-winning show dog, popularly known as the winery's "retired supermodel," Stormy lives a peaceful life, napping at the heels of wine drinkers in the tasting room or on the cool floor near the tanks, often with a squeaky plastic boot in her mouth. Despite the property's alluring acres of Sangiovese, Zinfandel, and other varietals, she prefers to stay close to her home base—allowing children to crawl all over her, employees to dress her in scarves and hats for special occasions, and everyone to pet her. On holidays when the winery is closed, general manager and winemaker Chris Dearden takes Stormy home, where she snuggles up to her granddaughter, Nera Bella, a name that means "black beauty" in Italian.

Lulu

LULU & BUCK
BERINGER VINEYARDS

Lulu, an eight-year-old black Labrador retriever, and Buck, a four-year-old yellow Labrador retriever, both hail from a farm in Eastern Montana. To Ron Schrieve, winemaker for the Beringer group, the dogs have an incredible talent: they announce precisely when the grapes are ready for harvest. As the grapes mature, they thoughtfully sniff the clusters, but it is only when the fruit is perfectly ripe that they actually start eating. Born without hip sockets, Lulu is nonetheless happy to run all day, chasing her Kong toy around the vineyards as if nothing is wrong. Buck, whose full name is Tie 'em Up Buckaroo because of his father's ability to bulldog cattle, ambles beside Lulu among the vines, content to run and evaluate all the grapes in the Beringer vineyards.

CRACKERS, LADDIE LU & CURBY
BREMER FAMILY WINERY

Winery owner Laura Bremer followed her dream when she and her husband, John, started their Napa Valley winery. Laura also made dreams come true for three dogs in desperate situations. "It's about the land, passion, love, caring, and helping out where we can," she says. Laddie Lu, a seven-year-old Labrador retriever mix, had a broken leg when Laura found her at a shelter. Curby, a six-year-old Labrador retriever mix, was kept in a small fenced backyard for years and given little attention before Laura came along. Crackers, a five-year-old Australian shepherd/Bernese mountain dog mix, needed extensive hip surgery and rehabilitation when he met Laura. Today, Laddie Lu gets so excited to meet winery guests that she carries her leash in her mouth and nudges people for petting. Curby, free of fences at last, runs wildly in the vineyard each day, and Crackers is happiest when he rides beside Laura in the Kubota ATV. All three dogs demonstrate the healing powers of winery life.

Curby

Laddie Lu

Crackers

Toffee (left),
Bandit & Cocoa

PORTO, BANDIT, COCOA & TOFFEE
BUEHLER VINEYARDS

Porto

Porto, an eleven-year-old Portuguese water dog, is an excellent greeter and guard dog with a talent for putting visitors at ease. Occasionally, when he's had his fill of food, he leads Bandit, a five-year-old miniature poodle, to the pond, and they return home wet and filthy. Together with the two energetic Shih Tzus, three-year-old Cocoa and two-year-old Toffee, the dogs roam the mountainous vineyards, taking in the scents of the ripening Cabernet Sauvignon and old-vine Zinfandel grapes and running until they're exhausted and ready for dinner. The Buehler estate has been featured in numerous publications, including catalogues for Eddie Bauer and Lands End, but the Buehlers are more excited that the dogs can enjoy this scenic property with them.

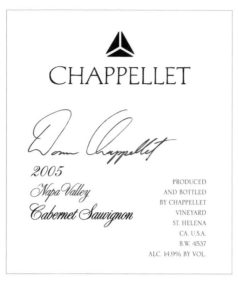

OMAR
CHAPPELLET VINEYARD & WINERY

In some ways, Omar, an eight-year-old Anatolian shepherd, behaves the way he is expected to. At 160 pounds, he is intimidating in size and temperament, protective of his family and the property. Anatolians were bred to guard goats and sheep in Turkey, and Omar—in an odd twist—has adopted winery owner Cyril Chappellet as his "flock," both protecting and respecting him. Proudly sporting a dog tag that reads "Canine Sommelier," from Blakesley Chappellet's Dogs Uncorked line of dog products, Omar is an essential part of the winery. In his domain on Pritchard Hill, he's content to keep Cyril company in the office, ride shotgun in the 1960 customized Land Cruiser used for winery tours, or sit on the porch to welcome visitors. Those who know Omar best are humored by his unique way of showing affection, vigorously nuzzling their head and neck.

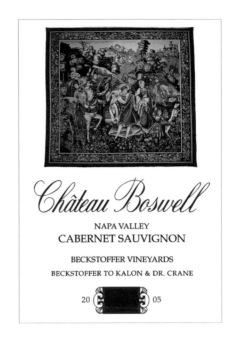

Château Boswell

NAPA VALLEY
CABERNET SAUVIGNON

BECKSTOFFER VINEYARDS
BECKSTOFFER TO KALON & DR. CRANE

20 05

JOHN ROBIE & JACKSON
CHATEAU BOSWELL WINERY

Jackson

John Robie, a five-year-old golden retriever, was named after the jewel burglar played by Cary Grant in *To Catch a Thief.* "Although he is handsome, he's not sly," says winery owner Susan Boswell, thanks in part to his excellent dog training by Brandt Wilson of Top Dawgs. He is generally well-behaved—treading carefully through the obsidian, volcanic ash and numerous Indian arrowheads on the property and eventually coming home relatively calm and clean. But when his favorite visitor, Jackson—Jacquelynn and Josh Peeples' very persuasive ten-year-old black Labrador retriever—leads him to the pond to swim, the dogs won't come out until they're dragged out. And of course both emerge covered in green slime, refreshed and happy to shake themselves dry and move on to the next adventure.

Maya

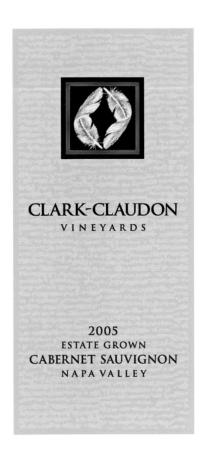

CLARK-CLAUDON
VINEYARDS

2005
ESTATE GROWN
CABERNET SAUVIGNON
NAPA VALLEY

MAYA & IZZY
CLARK - CLAUDON VINEYARDS

Izzy

Izzy, a two-year-old Havanese, is a gentle companion and a shadow to vineyard owner Laurie Claudon, accompanying her at the winery and everywhere else. She loves the back of the couch, empty car seats, and the safety of sturdy chairs, but her favorite place is in Laurie's lap, resting her chin on her shoulder. Maya, a three-month-old black Labrador retriever, is Izzy's opposite. Whether she's splashing in a bucket, eating burritos with the vineyard workers, or biting a vacuum cleaner cord in half, she is nearly always in motion. Already attached to vineyard owner Tom Clark, she puts her head on his shoulder when he's driving. When Tom is away, she sits patiently on his boots, longing for his company just as Mia, her beloved predecessor, once did.

2 0 0 1

CORISON

KRONOS VINEYARD

NAPA VALLEY

CABERNET
SAUVIGNON

ALC 13.8% BY VOL

PUCK & EMMA
CORISON WINERY

A happy pair, Puck and Emma fit right in at the winery. Cathy Corison has lived with dogs at her winery for thirty years, and whether she's creating wine at her gray barn or enjoying her family at home, she can't imagine her life without dogs by her side. Puck, a five-year-old collie, was bred to herd and is therefore talented at keeping the family together. Emma, a two-year-old Bernese mountain dog, was trained at obedience school and then by Puck. Together, Puck and Emma roam in the vineyards and come running when they hear Cathy or her husband, William Martin, calling them. Active and affectionate, they're always thrilled to see family, friends, and visitors.

*Puck (left) &
Emma*

EHLERS
ESTATE
— 2005 —
CABERNET SAUVIGNON
ST. HELENA
NAPA VALLEY

RIPLEY
EHLERS ESTATE

Ripley, an eight-year-old Australian shepherd, is a big-hearted dog with an even bigger appetite. As soon as he arrives at the winery each day with winemaker Rudy Zuidema, he makes his rounds, checking in with everyone at the office and hoping for a treat. At 9:45 a.m., he heads to the vineyard to share a taco with the crew. Ripley's inner clock tells him when every employee takes a break, so no one is surprised when he shows up for a snack. Always grateful, Ripley thanks everyone by jumping up to kiss their faces.

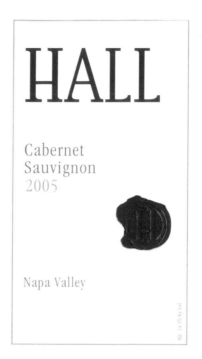

HALL

Cabernet
Sauvignon
2005

Napa Valley

THOMAS & MR. BIGGLES
HALL WINERY

Thomas

Mr. Biggles, a four-year-old English mastiff named after a British cartoon character, is happiest when he's lying on the cool tasting room floor with his nose between his paws—a pose that Neil Bason, in guest relations, says is the dog's "top speed." Motivated to move only by something tasty, he has been known to steal food from desks in the back room, leaving a telltale trail of drool out the door. Thomas, a two-year-old Cavalier King Charles spaniel, is the foil to Mr. Biggles, preferring not to sleep or to snatch unattended food but to greet guests with excitement and then run into the lovely courtyard to chase birds. Hospitality manager Katie Sieu, whose muffins have fallen victim to Mr. Biggles, says that Thomas nips at the bigger dog's heels hoping for a game of chase, but Mr. Biggles will have none of that.

Mr. Biggles

Delilah (left),
Miss Ellie & JoJo

GABBY, SKIP, DELILAH, JOJO & MISS ELLIE

KELHAM VINEYARDS

Skip (front) &
Gabby

At Kelham Vineyards & Winery, the dogs are a cast of whimsical characters in an energetic play. Skip, the eight-year-old Jack Russell "terrorist," swims, runs, and makes a racket, getting everyone riled up before he trots home. JoJo, a seven-year-old American bulldog, gets so excited when he plays with winemaker Hamilton Nicholsen that he dances along the edge of the pool before plunging in with a belly flop and biting on the waves he's made. Gabby, a three-year-old black Labrador retriever, appears to have "nipple anxiety," say winery owners Rawson and Susanna Kelham, because she's always running with something in her mouth. Delilah, a one-year-old French bulldog, likes to splash around the pool alone before following office manager Shannon More to the tasting room for fallen leftovers. Miss Ellie, a one-year-old Rhodesian Ridgeback/coonhound mix, is the new dog at the estate, slowly coming into her own. Despite their eccentricities, all the dogs thrive—interacting continually with family and guests—in the idyllic winery setting.

Pilot

Pilot (left), Lily
& Panchita

PILOT, PANCHITA & LILY
KULETO ESTATE FAMILY VINEYARDS

Panchita

Panchita, Lily, and Pilot are full of boundless energy, providing constant entertainment for Pat Kuleto and his son, Daniel. Panchita, a seven-year-old Labrador retriever/Border collie mix, is the estate's tour guide. When she's not running in circles around guests, she's awing them with her water ballet routine, a complicated sequence involving hoses and spouts in the swimming pool. Lily, a four-year-old black Labrador retriever, is a compulsive hunter of duck, goose, and upland game. An admirable jumper and true gourmand, she jumps to the highest counters to taste fine cheeses, dried cured meats, and expensive caviar. Pilot, a three-year-old chocolate Labrador retriever, is the estate's greeter, goodwill ambassador, and occasional wedding-cake eater. His choice of cuisine—from dead mice to bloated frogs and even glass—has astounded and at times terrified the family. Despite any shocking habits, the three dogs are beloved by family, friends, and guests.

*Whiskey (left) &
Patty*

PATTY & WHISKEY
LIVINGSTON MOFFETT WINERY

Patty and Whiskey, both nine-year-old Australian shepherds, are fearless hunters. They spend most of their hours tracking animal scents and return home dragging deer heads and squirrel carcasses. One day Patty chased a deer over the hill behind the winery and returned, breathless and happy, with a deep puncture wound in her chest, clearly the loser in a good fight. When the hunters are at home, winery owner John Livingston enjoys playing ball with Whiskey while Patty rests comfortably. Both dogs get along so well with guests and the winery's three cats that the casual observer would never suspect their unquenchable passion for the hunt.

Whiskey

Porcini

Figeac

PORCINI, FIGEAC & VOODOO
MERRYVALE VINEYARDS

At Merryvale, a dog-friendly winery, the thirteen-year-old Jack Russell terrier, Porcini, runs on the lawn and circles the edge of the refreshing fountain. Because he is feisty and fearless, hospitality coordinator and wine educator Sandra Barros needs to keep an eye on him, but she's grateful for his abilities as a watchdog, hiking partner, and lovable lapdog. "He so wonderful, I don't know why I waited so long to get a dog," she says. Figeac, a ten-year-old black Labrador retriever/Newfoundland mix, and Voodoo, a black Labrador retriever/Border collie mix, drink from the winery fountain but prefer running in the vineyards. Rene and Laurence Schlatter, who operate the winery with their family, chose Figeac from the Napa shelter and Voodoo from a rescue group in Woodland. While Figeac chases rabbits, Voodoo steals the children's toys and trains for half-marathons with Laurence. Since they are so active, they often get special treats from their favorite restaurant, Taylor's Refresher.

Voodoo

2 0 0 4

PROFILE
MERRYVALE

NAPA VALLEY

RED WINE

PRODUCT OF USA

ALC. 14.5% BY VOL.

SARA
PARRY CELLARS

Sara, a seven-year-old mix, was found wandering on a roadside in Calistoga when a shelter took her in. Perhaps part German shepherd, part Labrador retriever, and part Weimaraner, she has confounded everyone who tries to uncover her heritage. "Only her mother knows for sure," say winery owners Sue and Stephen Parry. Luckily, she's a perfect fit for the Parrys, whether she's keeping them company in the office, digging for gophers in the vineyard's rocky soil, or welcoming friends who visit and taste their limited releases of Cabernet Sauvignon. An alert watchdog, she continually scans the property even as the sun sets over the Mayacamas Mountains. Her deep attachment to her home has kept her from wanting to walk the streets again.

Liberty (left) &
Sadie

SADIE & LIBERTY
RAYMOND VINEYARDS

For Sadie, a three-year-old black Labrador retriever, and Liberty, a five-year-old yellow Labrador retriever, nothing is more important than catching a stick. Of course, they love racing through the long-established family vineyards of Cabernet Sauvignon and Merlot grapes; they love kind words and affection wherever they can get them; and because they're Labs, they love a good meal. But as soon as a stick is tossed into the sparkling cool reservoir, all thoughts of grapevines, love, and food vanish as they compete to fetch the wonderful stick. Liberty, who is bigger, can often muscle his way to victory, but Sadie, who is quick and agile, wins the prize almost as often. Vineyard manager Craig Raymond has never been able to cure them of their obsession with sticks, so he tries to amass a ready supply in the morning.

Moose Rombauer
Winery Greeter

TELEPHONE 707-963-5170   WINE ORDERS 800-622-2206
FACSIMILE 707-963-5752   www.rombauervineyards.com
3522 Silverado Trail · St. Helena · California 94574

MOOSE
ROMBAUER VINEYARDS

Moose, a six-year-old chocolate Labrador retriever, is a gentle soul, spending most of his time strolling through the wooded property, socializing in the tasting room, and napping in the office. One day, when a summer employee brought orphaned young kittens to the office to bottle-feed them during her breaks, the 100-pound Moose sauntered over and licked one of the kittens lovingly, even though the 4.3-ounce kitten was the size of Moose's nose. Winery owners Koerner and Joan Rombauer adopted Moose three years ago from a military couple who had to ship out just before the war. Another couple adopted Moose's brother, Travis. Recently, Moose and Travis were reunited for a visit. When they met again, at last, their hair stood on end and they circled each other for a while. Then something clicked and they became ecstatic, jumping and yelping. The Rombauers had never seen Moose so excited!

Tosca

TOSCA & CHARLIE
RustRidge Ranch and Winery

Tosca and Charlie—yellow Labrador retrievers, ages eight and seven—are mother and son. They are RustRidge's celebrities, having been featured in the *San Francisco Chronicle*, *Bark* magazine, and two 2005 yellow Labrador retriever calendars. Yet their fame has not gone to their heads. Each day they greet guests and escort them down the long, winding driveway to the tasting room. They also herd the ranch horses to the fence so that visitors can pet them. When they sense that visitors are about to enjoy a picnic lunch, Tosca and Charlie quickly move under the picnic tables, politely waiting for anything that might come their way. Sometimes a ranch cat also drops by to check out the offerings. Winery owners Jim Fresquez and Susan Meyer encourage Tosca and Charlie to lead their bed-and-breakfast's guests on hikes through the vineyards and hills. In the evenings, Tosca and Charlie enjoy hanging out with the guests on the B&B's front porch—a fitting end to a great day on the ranch.

Charlie

Rusty

CJ

RUSTY, JACK, CJ & ADIA
SALVESTRIN ESTATE VINEYARD AND WINERY

Rusty, Jack, CJ, and Adia are full of energy all day. Rusty, a four-year-old golden retriever, and Jack and CJ, the seven-year-old and two-year-old Jack Russell terriers, chase rabbits in the vineyard for hours. When they've had enough, they rustle up Adia, a nine-week-old American white shepherd from Evansville, Illinois, to greet guests at the winery or historic bed-and-breakfast. The Salvestrin family was glad to see that Adia—who became attached to CJ within hours of meeting him—will now follow him anywhere. "Our dogs are part of our family," says Susanne Salvestrin. "At our family-owned winery, our dogs extend the warmth and hospitality we strive so hard to show our guests."

Jack

Mojo

MOJO & TACHE
S.E. CHASE FAMILY CELLARS

At age four, Tache—a smooth fox terrier—accompanies winemaker Nile Zacherle to work every day. Though he lost his foot in a vineyard accident, he hasn't slowed down at all, using his partial leg to kick off his running and fetching adventures. Even when he's poking his head deeply into gopher holes, he rushes to answer Nile's whistle. When he's swimming, however, he is deaf to all calls. Only when Nile drives slowly away does Tache panic and jump, soaking wet, into Nile's truck. Mojo, an eleven-month-old cockapoo, is happiest in the arms of winery owner Pam Simpson or her kids, Ben and Abby. When he wants to get down, he leaps dramatically into the air and runs through the vineyards, eating grapes or simply rolling in a pile of fresh grapeskins, thoroughly rubbing his ears against them. At home he coos like a bird, steals socks, and indulges his family as they dress him up in Build-A-Bear clothes and holiday T-shirts.

Tache

SPOTTSWOODE

2005

Family Estate Grown
CABERNET SAUVIGNON

SW

Spottswoode Estate Vineyard & Winery
St·HELENA·NAPA VALLEY

Alc. 14.1% by Vol.

MURPHY & RILEY
SPOTTSWOODE ESTATE VINEYARD & WINERY

Riley

Murphy, a three-year-old black Labrador retriever who can't stop feasting on Spottswoode's delicious organic grapes, gained eleven pounds during the last harvest. Riley, a one-year-old black Labrador retriever, occasionally distracts Murphy from eating by stealing Murphy's bones and hiding them in the garden. To winery owner Mary Novak's displeasure, Riley also chews the dog beds, as well as her grandchildren's toys, no matter how many bones he steals. Luckily for Mary and her daughter, Beth Novak Milliken, Riley also loves to run, so he stays out of trouble whenever he runs with Murphy in the vineyard. Of course, eventually he makes his way home for more chewing.

192

Czor

TESSA, CZOR & ELVIS
V. SATTUI WINERY

Tessa and Czor, both age four, and Elvis, three, come from a German line of Bernese mountain dogs and serve as the winery's most visible ambassadors. President Tom Davies takes one each day to the office with him and gets stopped wherever he goes along the way—in the deli, in the tasting room, or on the picnic grounds. Tessa, who was chosen from the litter for her gregariousness, is always excited to meet hundreds of guests a day and to occasionally snatch a salami from someone's shopping basket. Czor, says Tom's wife, Cara Davies, is their quiet, easygoing "big boy" and prefers never to leave Tom's side. Elvis came to them with a heart defect, but since a valve was repaired in surgery, he's become energetic, hilarious, and excellent company for Tessa and Czor. Though Tom admires their marketing abilities, he rarely brings all three to work at once. If he does, he's sorry. "Their popularity makes it impossible to get office work done," he says, shaking his head.

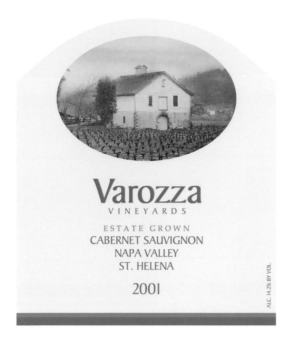

Varozza
VINEYARDS
ESTATE GROWN
CABERNET SAUVIGNON
NAPA VALLEY
ST. HELENA

2001

ALC. 14.2% BY VOL.

LUCY
VAROZZA VINEYARDS

Lucy, a two-year-old German shorthaired pointer, spends her days running. Rabbits don't have a chance to feast on the vines when Lucy's there, running and barking until they're gone. When the vineyard is free of intruders, she swims vigorously in the pond to cool down. All of this activity gives Lucy a voracious appetite, and winery owners Jack, Dianna, and Jason Varozza have learned the hard way that her appetite has no bounds. As a puppy, she grabbed a prime rib off the counter and pranced proudly into the living room to show off the giant piece of meat in her mouth. Months later, Dianna roasted a large chicken and left briefly to answer the phone. When she returned, Lucy had the chicken in her mouth—but she wasn't eating it. She was crying because she had just eaten her dinner and was too full for the chicken. These days, Lucy likes to find a spot at home where she can keep an eye on every member of the family—probably for the food opportunities, Dianna says.

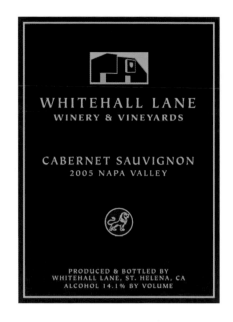

BRUNO
WHITEHALL LANE WINERY

Bruno, a one-year-old standard poodle, is not yet as famous as Timber, the cover dog for the first edition of *Winery Dogs of Napa Valley*, but he's on his way. The perfect height for counter-surfing, Bruno will steal anything edible from the bar, so winery owners Tom and Jakki Leonardini are always on the lookout. One day Tom set down his favorite meal, a bone-in rib eye, on the counter and turned away for just a second. A second is all Bruno needed, though, to snatch the steak and run out back for a feast. Companionable as well as sly, Bruno loves to sit beside Jakki in the car and dance at home with Julia, the couple's adoring eight-year-old daughter.

Stags Leap

Cliff Lede Vineyards

Clos Du Val

Darioush

Regusci Winery

Shafer Vineyards

Signorello Vineyards

Silverado Vineyards

Yountville

Domaine Chandon

Hopper Creek Winery

Louisa

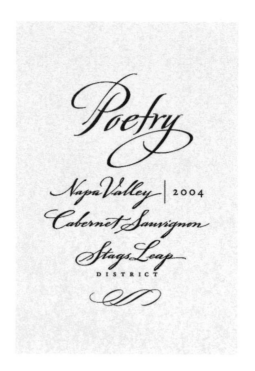

TRUFFLES, LOUISA &
LORD WENSLEYDALE
CLIFF LEDE VINEYARDS

The dogs at Cliff Lede—Truffles, a six-year-old French bulldog; Lord Wensleydale Francis Wigglesworth, a five-year-old English bulldog; and Miss Louisa Bell, a three-year-old bloodhound—bring their own brand of energy to the winery. Truffles, the ringbearer at the wedding of winemaker Michelle Edwards and viticulturist Dan Fischl, gets extremely excited whenever the television is on. Lord Wensleydale, known for his discerning palate, will moonwalk and huff until he's served a generous pour of a fine Burgundy. Louisa, true to her breed, sniffs out the two worst winemakers' scourges—TCA in the cellar and powdery mildew in the vineyard. Together, the dogs enjoy roaming the grounds to the winery, tasting room, and art gallery on opening nights, where they all hope cheese will come their way.

Lord Wensleydale (left),
Louisa & Truffles

ALFIE
CLOS DU VAL

At Clos Du Val, guests come to sip delicious wines at the tables and stroll the beautiful grounds, enjoying the sunshine and good company. But when Alfie arrives, everyone scrambles for their cameras. A four-year-old royal standard poodle with a magisterial walk, Alfie is a star in the valley. And while guests wish he would stay all day, Alfie has important duties forcing him to go. As a therapy dog in a convalescent home in Sonoma, he visits dozens of residents, encouraging interaction and lifting their spirits. In the Barks & Books program at the Napa City-County Library, Alfie is a certified reading education assistant dog—a profession that assistant tasting room manager Rose Galanty says is "a perfect fit." Children who struggle with reading line up to reserve a time to read to Alfie. "Whenever kids are around, he ignores me completely," Rose says, and that's just what kids want—instant love and rapt attention as they read their books.

Jacques

CHU CHU & JACQUES
DARIOUSH

At Darioush, it is not unusual to see a dog running upon the lavish estate or napping in the back offices. Employees are free to bring dogs to work, a policy that makes life exciting for Chu Chu, a two-year-old Lhasa apso, and his best pal, Jacques, a two-year-old standard poodle. Winemaker Steve Devitt walks with them in the vineyards, where Chu Chu enjoys the fresh scents and Jacques keeps an eye out for rabbits. Though both were bred to be show dogs, they spend their afternoons running on the great front lawn and napping in Steve's truck—unaware that they are a testament to their breeds. In the lab, where the floor is cool, Steve's colleagues can't resist petting them and giving them a variety of treats.

Chu Chu

Andy (front) &
Trixie

Haas & Scrappy

ANDY, TRIXIE, HAAS & SCRAPPY
REGUSCI WINERY

She's only two feet tall, but few would argue that Trixie, or "Princess," as she prefers to be called, presides over Regusci Winery with a keen eye and a benevolent paw. Her entourage includes three male dogs. Andy, also a Welsh Corgi, acts as sentry and protector, ensuring everyone's safety under his watch. Haas and Scrappy, six-year-old yellow Labrador retrievers, provide muscle for the big jobs: inspecting limousines and announcing new guests as they arrive. Together, Princess and her boys are the consummate canine hospitality team. As Will Rogers once said, "If there are no dogs in Heaven, then when I die I want to go where they went." Trixie, Andy, Haas, and Scrappy already believe they're in heaven.

Andy & Trixie

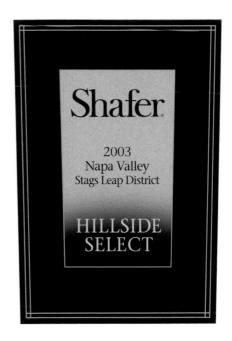

TUCKER
SHAFER VINEYARDS

Tucker, an eight-year-old yellow Labrador retriever, is winery owner John Shafer's third Labrador. Jake, a black Lab, loved to swim, and Rocky, a yellow Lab, spent his old age showing the young Tucker around. Tucker's arrival at the winery is heralded in the timeline of important dates posted in the office—in 1998, it is proclaimed, "John brings new puppy Tucker to the office, where he joins John's phone conversations and eats the mail." Today Tucker leaves John's mail alone, barking at the delivery trucks, devouring grapes, and greeting visitors. There's a sculpture of a Labrador on the front step, but it's hard to look at it long when Tucker is clamoring to say hello.

Zizou

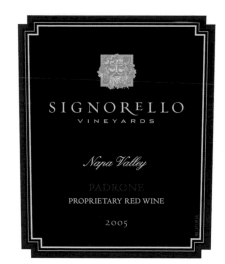

BANDIT & ZIZOU
SIGNORELLO VINEYARDS

Intelligent and driven, Bandit—a ten-year-old Brittany spaniel and champion show dog— understands English and French and is excellent with visitors and children. During the day, Bandit often runs free in a fenced twenty-acre vineyard, checking vines one by one, chasing rabbits, and pointing to quail. An astute bird dog, he also hunts with winemaker Pierre Birebent, pointing and fetching reliably. Zizou—an eighteen-month-old Brittany spaniel—shares a grandfather with Bandit and is named for a famous French soccer player. Like Bandit, he loves to run at full speed in the vineyards. During his first hunting trip with Pierre, he expertly pointed to a bird but was not yet able to fetch it. Today, however, he is an accomplished bird dog and valued family member.

Bandit

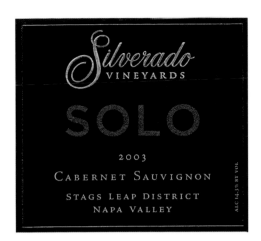

LULU LOUISE
SILVERADO VINEYARDS

Lulu Louise, a ten-year-old black Labrador retriever/German shorthaired pointer mix, spends each morning lazing on the couch, gently gumming her fuzzy toys and snacking on juicy avocados and tomatoes. In the afternoons, winemaker Jonathan Emmerich takes her to the vineyards, where she glides effortlessly under the guide wires and drip lines. An accomplished hunter, she burrows her nose deeply into the ground and lifts it out, sneezing—sometimes with a gopher or mole to show off. Though not fond of other dogs, tall people, or walking on sidewalks, she is at ease wading in the Napa River and relaxing with her trusted family and friends.

Ally

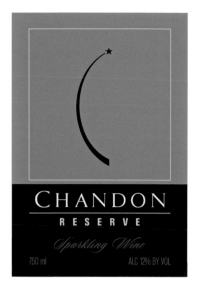

ALLY & GUNNER
DOMAINE CHANDON

Ally, a liver German shorthaired pointer, was about to be put down at a shelter in Michigan when Rick Aldine, director of winegrowing, found her online. Rick bought her a ticket, met her at the airport, and spent the next two years training her to be an excellent hunter. Just as Rick had hoped, she was soon holding a point quietly whenever he hunted pheasants and quail. When Ally's beloved canine hunting companion, Bullet, suddenly died, she took it hard. Permanent spots appeared on her coat, and she withdrew from social situations. Today, thanks to the happy-go-lucky five-month-old silver Labrador retriever, Gunner, she has started to come out of her shell. At the vineyards she has shown Gunner how to chase deer and dig for gophers. And while Gunner runs all day, Ally likes to take breaks in the back of Rick's truck, her safe haven.

Csavo

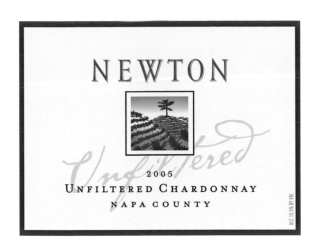

HOBS & CSAVO
DOMAINE CHANDON

Hobs

Hobs and Csavo, the winery's two Hungarian vizslas, are fast and athletic—perfect companions for senior relationship marketing manager Emily Oakes and her husband, Jonathan. Together, they hike in the woods and the dogs run with speed and grace while the Oakes are skiing and mountain biking. At four years old, Hobs, a Chicago native, loves traveling and will gladly withstand the cold winter temperatures of the Pacific to get in a good swim. Csavo, whose name means "dude" in Hungarian, is just ten weeks old, but already he has no trouble keeping pace with Hobs, his favorite playmate.

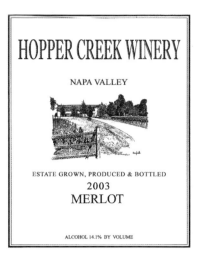

HOPPER CREEK WINERY

NAPA VALLEY

ESTATE GROWN, PRODUCED & BOTTLED
2003
MERLOT

ALCOHOL 14.1% BY VOLUME

Chili

CHILI & DUNCAN
HOPPER CREEK WINERY

The dogs at Hopper Creek will do anything for love. Chili, a five-year-old Border collie/Doberman pinscher mix, came to retail sales manager Dan Blach and his daughter, Emily, from the Napa Humane Society, eager for affection. Today, as guests in the tasting room try an array of complex wines, Chili rolls onto his back for a belly rub—not caring if he rolls onto someone's feet. Duncan, a three-year-old Australian shepherd/Border collie mix, is nicknamed "Love More" because he boldly nudges people to pet him or throw a ball for a game of fetch. Assistant cellar master Joseph Ferraro says that even after Duncan was hit by a car while chasing a deer across a highway, he begged Joseph to throw a ball, not seeming to mind his broken foot.

Duncan

WINERY LISTING

Acacia Vineyard   (page 32)
2750 Las Amigas Road, Napa, CA 94559
(707) 226-9991
acacia.info@acaciavineyard.com
www.acaciawinery.com
Tasting by Appointment, Mon-Sat 10-4, Sun 12-4

Altamura Winery and Vineyards   (page 52)
1700 Wooden Valley Road, Napa Valley, CA 94558
(707) 253-2000
altamurawinery@aol.com
www.altamura.com
Tasting by Appointment, Mon-Fri 10-3

Anomaly Vineyards   (page 148)
P.O. Box 741, St. Helena, CA 94574
(707) 967-8448
anomalyvin@aol.com
www.anomalyvineyards.com

Behrens & Hitchcock   (page 122)
P.O. Box 1127, Calistoga, CA 94515
info@behrensandhitchcock.com
www.behrensandhitchcock.com

Benessere Vineyards   (page 150)
1010 Big Tree Road, St. Helena, CA 94574
(707) 963-5853
info@benesserevineyards.com
www.benesserevineyards.com
Open Tasting, Daily 10-5

Beringer Vineyards   (page 152)
2000 Main Street, St. Helena, CA 94574
(707) 967-4412
www.beringer.com
Open Tasting, Daily 10-5 (Winter), 10-6 (Summer)

Bouchaine Vineyards   (page 34)
1075 Buchli Station Road, Napa, CA 94559
(800) 654-WINE
info@bouchaine.com
www.bouchaine.com
Open Tasting, Daily 10:30-4

Bremer Family Winery   (page 154)
975 Deer Park Road, St. Helena, CA 94574
(707) 963-5411
sales@bremerfamilywinery.com
www.bremerfamilywinery.com
Tasting by Appointment, Daily 10-5

Buehler Vineyards   (page 156)
820 Greenfield Road, St. Helena, CA 94574
(707) 963-2155
buehlers@pacbell.net
www.buehlervineyards.com
Tasting by Appointment, Mon-Fri 10-4

Buena Vista Carneros Winery   (page 36)
18000 Old Winery Road, Sonoma, CA 95476
(800) 926-1266
bvw_info@buenavistawinery.com
www.buenavistawinery.com
Open Tasting, Mon-Fri 10-5, Sat-Sun 10-5:30

Cain Vineyard & Winery   (page 124)
3800 Langtry Road, St. Helena, CA 94574
(707) 963-1616
winery@cainfive.com
www.cainfive.com
Tasting by Appointment, Scheduled Twice Weekly

Castello di Amòrosa   (page 12)
4045 North St. Helena Highway, Calistoga, CA 94515
(707) 967-6272
tours@castellodiamorosa.com
www.castellodiamorosa.com
Open Tasting, Daily 9:30-6 (9:30-5, Dec-Feb 15)

Ceja Vineyards   (page 38)
1016 Las Amigas Road, Napa, CA 94559
(707) 255-3954 or (877) 633-3954
wine@cejavineyards.com
www.cejavineyards.com
Tasting by Appointment

Chappellet Vineyard & Winery   (page 158)
1581 Sage Canyon Road, St. Helena, CA 94574
(800) 4 - WINERY (494-6379)
toursandtastings@chappellet.com
www.chappellet.com
www.dogsuncorked.com
Tasting by Reservation, Mon-Sat

Chateau Boswell Winery   (page 160)
3468 Silverado Trail, St. Helena, CA 94574
(707) 963-5472
josh@chateauboswellwinery.com
www.chateauboswellwinery.com
Tasting by Appointment

Clark - Claudon Vineyards   (page 162)
wine@clarkclaudon.com
www.clarkclaudon.com

Cliff Lede Vineyards   (page 200)
1473 Yountville Cross Road, Yountville, CA 94599
(800) 428-2259
tastingroom@cliffledevineyards.com
www.cliffledevineyards.com
Open Tasting, Daily 10-5

Clos Du Val   (page 202)
5330 Silverado Trail, Napa, CA 94558
(707) 261-5200
cdv@closduval.com
www.closduval.com
Open Tasting, Daily 10-5

CONSTANT–Diamond Mountain Vineyard & Winery   (page 28)
2121 Diamond Mountain Road, Calistoga, CA 94515
(707) 942-0707
info@constantwine.com
www.constantwine.com
Wild Rides and Tasting by Appointment

Corison Winery   (page 164)
987 St. Helena Highway, St. Helena, CA 94574
(707) 963-0826
bob@corison.com
www.corison.com
Tasting by Appointment, Daily 10-5

Darioush   (page 204)
4240 Silverado Trail, Napa, CA 94558
(707) 257-2345
info@darioush.com
www.darioush.com
Open Tasting, Daily 10:30-5

Delectus Winery   (page 14)
908 Enterprise Way #C, Napa, CA 94558
(707) 255-1252
New winery opening 2011:
15300 Ida Clayton Road, Calistoga, CA 95448
admin@delectuswinery.com
www.delectuswinery.com
Tasting by Appointment, Mon-Fri

Domaine Chandon   (page 214)
1 California Drive, Yountville, CA 94599
(707) 944-2280
customerservice@chandon.com
www.chandon.com
Open Tasting, Daily 10-6 (10-7, Fri-Sun, May-Oct)

Domaine Charbay Winery & Distillery   (page 126)
4001 Spring Mountain Road, St. Helena, CA 94574
(800) 634-7845
info@charbay.com
www.charbay.com
Visits by Appointment, Mon-Sat

Domaine La Due   (page 54)
1623 Bryce Court, Napa, CA 94558
(866) 383-9463
angela@domaineladue.com
www.domaineladue.com
Private Tasting Available

Dutch Henry Winery   (page 16)
4310 Silverado Trail, Calistoga, CA 94515
(888) 224-5879
info@dutchhenry.com
www.dutchhenry.com
Tasting by Appointment, Daily 10-5

Ehlers Estate   (page 166)
3222 Ehlers Lane, St. Helena, CA 94574
(707) 963-5972
info@ehlersestate.com
www.ehlersestate.com
Open Tasting, Daily 10-5

Elkhorn Peak Cellars   (page 56)
200 Polson Road, P.O. Box 821, Napa, CA 94558
(888) 829-5082
www.elkhornpeakcellars.com

Elyse Winery   (page 58)
2100 Hoffman Lane, Napa, CA 94558
(707) 944-2900
info@elysewinery.com
www.elysewinery.com
Tasting by Appointment

Envy Wines   (page 18)
1170 Tubbs Lane, Calistoga, CA 94515
(707) 942-4670
info@envywines.com
www.envywines.com
Tasting by Appointment, 10-4:30

Esser Vineyards   (page 60)
4040 Spring Mountain Road, St. Helena, CA 94574
(707) 963-1300
info@esservineyards.com
www.esservineyards.com
Tasting by Appointment at 205-B Jim Oswald Way in American Canyon

Etude Wines   (page 40)
1250 Cuttings Wharf Road, Napa, CA 94559
(707) 257-5300
etudeinfo@etudewines.com
www.etudewines.com
Open Tasting, Sat 11-4
Tasting by Appointment, Mon-Fri 10,1 and 3

Fleury Estate Winery   (page 94)
950 Galleron Road, Rutherford, CA 94573
(707) 967-8333
brian@fleurywinery.com
www.fleurywinery.com
Tasting by Appointment, Daily 10-4

Frazier Winery   (page 62)
40 Lupine Hill Road, Napa, CA 94558
(707) 255-3444
sales@frazierwinery.com
www.frazierwinery.com
Tasting by Appointment, Mon-Fri 8:30-6, Sat 9-5

Gargiulo Vineyards   (page 76)
575 Oakville Cross Road, Napa, CA 94558
(707) 944-2770
sharon@gargiulovineyards.com
www.gargiulovineyards.com
Tasting by Appointment

Graeser Estate & Winery   (page 20)
255 Petrified Forest Road, Calistoga, CA 94515
(707) 942-4437
richard@graeserwinery.com
www.graeserwinery.com

Grgich Hills Cellar   (page 96)
1829 St. Helena Hwy, Rutherford, CA 94573
(800) 532-3057
info@grgich.com
www.grgich.com
Open Tasting, Daily 9:30-4:30

Groth Vineyards & Winery   (page 78)
750 Oakville Cross Road, Oakville, CA 94562
(707) 944-0290
info@grothwines.com
www.grothwines.com
Tasting by Appointment, Mon-Sat 10-4

Guilliams Vineyards   (page 128)
3851 Spring Mountain Road, St. Helena, CA 94574
(707) 963-9059
www.guilliams.com
Tasting by Appointment

HALL Winery St. Helena   (page 168)
401 St. Helena Highway South, St. Helena, CA 94574
(707) 967-2626
info@hallwines.com
www.hallwines.com
Open Tasting, Daily 10-5:30

HALL Winery Rutherford
56 Auberge Road, Rutherford, CA 94573

Hess Collection Vineyards   (page 46)
4411 Redwood Road, Napa, CA 94558
(877) 707-HESS (4377)
info@hesscollection.com
www.hesscollection.com
Open Tasting, Daily 10-4

Honig Vineyard & Winery   (page 98)
850 Rutherford Road, Rutherford, CA 94573
(800) 929-2217
tastings@honigwine.com
www.honigwine.com
Tasting by Appointment, Daily 10-4

Hopper Creek Winery   (page 218)
6204 Washington Street, Yountville, CA 94558
(707) 944-0675
office@hoppercreek.com
www.hoppercreek.com
Tasting by Appointment, Tue-Sun 11-4

Juslyn Vineyards   (page 130)
2900 Spring Mountain Road, St. Helena, CA 94574
(707) 265-1804
info@juslynvineyards.com
www.juslynvineyards.com
Open Tasting at Silenus Tasting Room (Napa), Daily 10-4

Kelham Vineyards   (page 170)
360 Zinfandel Lane, St. Helena, CA 94574
(707) 963-2000
info@kelhamvineyards.com
www.kelhamvineyards.com
Tasting by Appointment

Kirkland Ranch Winery   (page 64)
One Kirkland Ranch Road, Napa, CA 94558
(707) 254-9100
info@kirklandranchwinery.com
www.kirklandranchwinery.com
Tasting by Appointment, 10-4

Kuleto Estate Family Vineyards   (page 172)
2470 Sage Canyon Road, St. Helena, CA 94574
(707) 963-9750
info@kuletoestate.com
www.kuletoestate.com
Tasting by Appointment, Mon-Sat 10:30 & 2:30

Livingston Moffett Winery   (page 174)
1895 Cabernet Lane, St. Helena, CA 94574
(800) 788-0370
info@livingstonwines.com
www.livingstonwines.com
Tasting by Appointment

Long Meadow Ranch Winery   (page 100)
P.O. Box 477, Rutherford, CA 94573
(707) 963-4555
info@longmeadowranch.com
www.longmeadowranch.com
Scenic Tours & Tasting by Appointment

Madonna Estate Winery   (page 42)
5400 Old Sonoma Road, Napa, CA 94559
(707) 255-8864
mail@madonnaestate.com
www.madonnaestate.com
Open Tasting, Daily 10-5

Merryvale Vineyards   (page 176)
1000 Main Street, St. Helena, CA 94574
(707) 963-7777
info@merryvale.com
www.merryvale.com
Open Tasting, Daily 10-6:30

Miner Family Vineyards   (page 80)
7850 Silverado Trail, Oakville, CA 94562
(800) 366-WINE (9463)
sales@minerwines.com
www.minerwines.com
Open Tasting, Daily 11-5

Miss Olivia Brion Pinot Noir   (page 66)
256 Franklin Street, Napa, CA 94559
(707) 287-2870
obrionwine@comcast.net
www.oliviabrion.com
Private Barrel Tasting by Appointment

Monticello Vineyards   (page 68)
4242 Big Ranch Road, Napa, CA 94558
(707) 253-2802
wine@corleyfamilynapavalley.com
www.corleyfamilynapavalley.com
Open Tasting, Daily 10-4:30

Oakville Ranch Vineyards   (page 82)
7781 Silverado Trail, Napa, CA 94558
(707) 944-9665
info@oakvilleranchvineyards.com
www.oakvilleranchvineyards.com
Open Tasting at Tasting on Main (St Helena), Daily 10:30-6

Outpost Estate Wines   (page 142)
2075 Summit Lake Drive, Angwin, CA 94508
(707) 965-1718
outpost@starband.net
www.outpostwines.com
Tasting by Appointment, Mon-Fri

Paloma Vineyard   (page 132)
4013 Spring Mountain Road, St. Helena, CA 94574
(707) 963-7504
info@palomavineyard.com
www.palomavineyard.com
Tasting by Appointment

Parry Cellars   (page 178)
3424 Silverado Trail North, St. Helena, CA 94574
(707) 967-8160
info@parrycellars.com
www.parrycellars.com
Tasting by Appointment

Plumpjack Winery   (page 84)
620 Oakville Cross Road, Oakville, CA 94562
(707) 945-1220
winery@plumpjack.com
www.plumpjack.com
Open Tasting, Daily 10-4

Provenance Vineyards   (page 102)
1695 St. Helena Highway, Rutherford, CA 94573
(707) 968-3633
info@provenancevineyards.com
www.provenancevineyards.com
Open Tasting, Daily 10-4:30

Quintessa   (page 104)
1601 Silverado Trail, Rutherford, CA 94573
(707) 967-1601
info@quintessa.com
www.quintessa.com
Tasting by Appointment, Daily 10-4

Ramian Estate Vineyards   (page 22)
5225 Solano Avenue, Napa, CA 94558
(707) 287-2721
info@ramianestate.com
www.ramianestate.com
Open Tasting at Silenus Tasting Room (Napa), Daily 10-4

Raymond Vineyards   (page 180)
849 Zinfandel Lane, St. Helena, CA 94574
(800) 525-2659
visitorcenter@raymondvineyards.com
www.raymondvineyards.com
Open Tasting, Daily 10-4

Regusci Winery   (page 206)
5584 Silverado Trail, Napa, CA 94558
(707) 254-0403
info@regusciwinery.com
www.regusciwinery.com
Tasting by Appointment, Daily 10-5

Robert Keenan Wincry   (page 134)
3660 Spring Mountain Road, St. Helena, CA 94574
(707) 963-9177
rkw@keenanwinery.com
www.keenanwinery.com
Open Tasting, Sat-Sun 11-4
Tasting by Appointment, Mon-Fri

Rombauer Vineyards   (page 182)
3522 Silverado Trail, St. Helena, CA 94574
(800) 622-2206
sheanar@rombauervineyards.com
www.rombauer.com
Open Tasting, Daily 10-5

Rubicon Estate   (page 106)
1991 St. Helena Highway, Rutherford, CA 94573
(707) 968-1161
tours@rubiconestate.com
www.rubiconestate.com
Open Tasting, Daily 10-5

Rudd Vineyards & Winery   (page 86)
500 Oakville Crossroad, Oakville, CA 94562
(707) 944-8577
info@ruddwines.com
www.ruddwines.com
Tasting by Appointment

RustRidge Ranch and Winery   (page 184)
2910 Lower Chiles Valley Road, St. Helena, CA 94574
(707) 965-9353
RustRidge@RustRidge.com
www.RustRidge.com
Open Tasting, Daily 10-4

Saddleback Cellars   (page 88)
7802 Money Road, Oakville, CA 94562
(707) 944-1305
hillery@saddlebackcellars.com
www.saddlebackcellars.com
Tasting by Appointment, Mon-Sat

Saintsbury   (page 44)
1500 Los Carneros Avenue, Napa, CA 94559
(707) 252-0592
info@saintsbury.com
www.saintsbury.com
Tasting by Appointment, Mon-Fri

Salvestrin Estate Vineyard and Winery   (page 186)
397 Main Street, St. Helena, CA 94574
(707) 963-5105
shannon@salvestrinwinery.com
www.salvestrinwinery.com
Tasting by Appointment

Schrader Vineyards   (page 70)
1271 Monticello Road, Napa, CA 94558
(707) 224-2599
info@schradervineyards.com
www.schradervineyards.com

Schweiger Vineyards   (page 136)
4015 Spring Mountain Road, St. Helena, CA 94574
(877) 963-4882
svwine@schweigervineyards.com
www.schweigervineyards.com
Tasting by Appointment

S.E. Chase Family Cellars   (page 188)
PO Box 508, St. Helena, CA 94574
(707) 963-1284
mail@chasecellars.com
www.chasecellars.com
Tasting by Appointment

Sequoia Grove Vineyards and Winery   (page 108)
8338 St. Helena Highway, Rutherford, CA 94558
(800) 851-7841
info@sequoiagrove.com
www.sequoiagrove.com
Open Tasting, Daily 10:30-5

Shafer Vineyards   (page 208)
6154 Silverado Trail, Napa, CA 94558
(707) 944-2877
info@shafervineyards.com
www.shafervineyards.com
Tasting by Appointment, Mon-Fri 10-2

Signorello Vineyards   (page 210)
4500 Silverado Trail, Napa, CA 94558
(707) 255-5990
info@signorellovineyards.com
www.signorellovineyards.com
Open Tasting, Daily 10:30-5

Silenus Vintners   (page 72)
5225 Solano Avenue, Napa, CA 94558
(707) 299-3930
tastingroom@silenusvintners.com
www.silenusvintners.com
Tasting by Appointment, Daily 10-4

Silverado Vineyards   (page 212)
6121 Silverado Trail, Napa, CA 94558
(707) 259-6611
rsparacio@silveradovineyards.com
www.silveradovineyards.com
Open Tasting, Daily 10-4:30

Spottswoode Estate Vineyard & Winery   (page 190)
1902 Madrona Avenue, St. Helena, CA 94574
(707) 963-0134
spottswoode@spottswoode.com
www.spottswoode.com
Tasting by Appointment, Tue & Fri at 10

Staglin Family Vineyard   (page 110)
P.O. Box 680, Rutherford, CA 94573
(707) 944-0477
info@staglinfamily.com
www.staglinfamily.com
Tasting by Appointment

Stony Hill Vineyard   (page 138)
P.O. Box 308, St. Helena, CA 94574
(707) 963-2636
www.stonyhillvineyard.com
Tasting by Appointment, Mon-Fri 9-5

Sullivan Vineyards   (page 112)
1090 Galleron Road, Rutherford, CA 94573
(877) 244-7337
www.sullivanwine.com
Tasting by Appointment, Daily 10-5

Swanson Vineyards   (page 114)
1271 Manley Lane, Rutherford, CA 94573
(707) 967-3500
salon@swansonvineyards.com
www.swansonvineyards.com
Tasting by Appointment, Wed-Sun

The Terraces   (page 116)
1450 Silverado Trail, St. Helena, CA 94574
(707) 963-1707
www.terraceswine.com
Tasting by Appointment

Trahan Winery   (page 118)
www.trahanwinery.com
chuck@trahanwinery.com
(707) 342-1364
Tasting by Appointment

Turnbull Wine Cellars   (page 90)
8210 St. Helena Highway, Oakville, CA 94562
(707) 963-5839
info@turnbullwines.com
www.turnbullwines.com
Open Tasting, Daily 10-4:30

V. Sattui Winery   (page 192)
1111 White Lane, St. Helena, CA 94574
(707) 963-7774
info@vsattui.com
www.vsattui.com
Open Tasting, Daily 9-5 (Winter), 9-6 (Summer)

Venge Vineyards   (page 144)
424 Crystal Springs Road, St. Helena, CA 94573
(707) 967-1008
info@vengevineyards.com
www.vengevineyards.com
Tasting by Appointment, Daily 10-5

Varozza Vineyards   (page 194)
514 Pratt Avenue, St. Helena, CA 94574
(707) 963-0331
www.varozzavineyards.com
Tasting by Appointment

Vincent Arroyo Winery   (page 24)
2361 Greenwood Avenue, Calistoga, CA 94515
(707) 942-6995
www.vincentarroyo.com
Open Tasting, Daily 10-4:30

Vineyard 7&8   (page 140)
4028 Spring Mountain Road, St. Helena, CA 94574
(707) 963-9425
info@vineyard7and8.com
www.vineyard7and8.com
Tasting by Appointment

Whitehall Lane Winery   (page 196)
1563 St. Helena Highway, St. Helena, CA 94574
(800) 963-9454
greatwine@whitehalllane.com
www.whitehalllane.com
Open Tasting, Daily 11-5:45

Zahtila Vineyards   (page 26)
2250 Lake County Highway, Calistoga, CA 94515
(707) 942-9251
sales@zahtilavineyards.com
www.zahtilavineyards.com
Tasting by Appointment

Winery Dogs photographer Heather Zundel relaxing with her children Zack (left), Shea & Jake

Kitty Crossing
Regusci Winery

Scenic Kuleto Estate Family Vineyards

Freddy Constant with Caso & Floozy
CONSTANT–Diamond Mountain Vineyard & Winery

Amelia Ceja
Ceja Vineyards

Riley fetching the paper
Acacia Vineyard

Winery Dogs cofounder, Allen Jacoby, hard at work

JoJo diving in for his daily swim
Kelham Vineyards

Distillery
Domaine Charbay Winery & Distillery

Sadie and Gary Koehler singing
Dutch Henry Winery

Tucker Crull & Curry
The Terraces

A non-canine friend
RustRidge Ranch and Winery

The Bartolucci Family
Madonna Estate Winery

Frank Altamura & Woody
Altamura Winery and Vineyards

Earl going for a ride
Bouchaine Vineyards

Winemaker Rudy Zuidema getting a kiss from Ripley
Ehlers Estate

Photography assistant Jake Zundel
Provenance Vineyards

Charlie
Juslyn Vineyards

Stormy
Benessere Vineyards
Photo courtesy of Kim Morse

Moxie sitting pretty
Envy Wines

Jake ready to lead the way for a tasting
Monticello Vineyards

Winery Dogs photographer Andrea Jacoby taking
a break with son, Andrew
Bouchaine Vineyards

Ludwig
Esser Vineyards

Lupo relaxing on the castle grounds
Castello di Amorosa

Laura Bremer with Crackers
Bremer Family Winery

J.
Vincent Arroyo Winery

Delilah (front) & Jojo
Kelham Vineyards

Louisa sniffing the vines
Cliff Lede Vineyards

Murphy
Spottswoode Estate Vineyard & Winery

Soda
Turnbull Wine Cellars

Scenic Madonna Estate

Bella with assistant winemaker Nate Page
The Terraces

Chou Mei Mei
Groth Vineyards & Winery

ACKNOWLEDGMENTS & PHOTO CREDITS

We are so thankful for the ongoing support of our families and friends as we continue this wonderful venture. I am also grateful for my son, Andrew, for being such a flexible and happy young traveler. I would like to give special thanks to Jaime Fritsch for his stunning photos and creative help editing and constructing version two; Luz Ovalle for her patience, friendship, and great photos; and Marci Grant, the baby whisperer, for her assistance and companionship. Elaine Riordan wishes to thank Ron Thomson for his excellent ideas and continual support, and Pops, a constant reminder that a happy dog can transform even a bad day into a perfect day.

Jaime Fritsch is a dog-loving freelance photographer based in Southern California. His photos are included on pages 64-65, 136-137, 142-143, and 216-217. Jaime's work is also featured in the soon-to-be-released *Winery Dogs of Central California*.

www.jaimefritsch.com

Luz Ovalle is a freelance photographer and graphic designer based in London. Her work is featured on pages 25, 73, 169, 183, 230 (Jake), and 231 (J.J.).

Photos on pages 70-71 courtesy of Danielle Pacheco

Photos on pages 108-109 courtesy of Matt McMann